MEDIA CASEBOOK

AN INTRODUCTORY READER IN AMERICAN MASS COMMUNICATIONS

Edited by

Peter M. Sandman
The Ohio State University

David M. Rubin
New York University
at Washington Square

David B. Sachsman
Rutgers—The State University
Livingston College

PRENTICE-HALL, INC., ENGLEWOOD CLIFFS, N.J.

ISBN: 0–13–572438–4
Library of Congress Catalog Card Number: 76–39316

10 9 8 7 6 5 4 3 2 1

Printed in the United States of America

PRENTICE-HALL INTERNATIONAL, INC., London
PRENTICE-HALL OF AUSTRALIA, PTY. LTD., Sydney
PRENTICE-HALL OF CANADA, LTD., Toronto
PRENTICE-HALL OF INDIA PRIVATE LIMITED, New Delhi
PRENTICE-HALL OF JAPAN, INC., Tokyo

Contents

Preface, xi

Introduction, 1

Robert L. Duffus, "To the Highest Bidder"
(Reprinted from the **New Republic**)

PART ONE

DEVELOPMENT, 7

1 Development, 9

"Covering the Nominating Conventions,
1844–1968" (Reprinted from the New
York **Herald,** the San Francisco **Daily
Examiner,** the New York **Tribune,** the
New York **Times,** the Los Angeles **Times,**
and **Miami and the Siege of Chicago** by
Norman Mailer)

PART TWO

RESPONSIBILITY, 27

2   *Self-Control* [*Ethics*] , 29

Noel Epstein, "Capital Newsmen Often
Play a Role in Creating the Events They
Cover" (Reprinted from the **Wall Street
Journal**)

3   *Internal Control* [*Gatekeeping*] , 37

Frank Allen Philpot, "The Making of a
Newscast" (Previously unpublished)

4   *Monopoly Control,* 48

Daniel J. Leab, "A Genealogy of the New
York Merger" (Reprinted from the
Columbia Journalism Review)

5   *Advertiser Control,* 56

Steve Knoll, "Sponsor Rules in ABC
Docus" (Reprinted from **Variety**)

6   *Source Control* [*News Management*] , 64

"The Pentagon Papers and the New York
Times" (Reprinted from **United States
Reports** and the New York **Times**)

7   *Government Control* [*Law*] , 75

"The Government Versus WBBM-TV"
(Reprinted from **Variety**)

8   *Public Control,* 91

KTAL-TV, "Statement of Policy" and
"Agreement" (Reprinted from **The Alfred
I. duPont-Columbia University Survey of
Broadcast Journalism 1968–1969,** edited
by Marvin Barrett)

PART THREE

MEDIA, 97

9   The Medium
and the Message, 99

Penn Kimball, "People Without Papers"
(Reprinted from **Public Opinion
Quarterly**)

10   Newspapers, 108

David L. Grey, "Decision-Making by a
Reporter Under Deadline Pressure"
(Reprinted from **Journalism Quarterly**)

11   Magazines, 118

Lee Nourse Patterson, "For Hopeful
Husband Hunters, Helen Gurley Brown
Has the Answers" (Reprinted from
Magazines in America—1968)

12   Broadcasting, 124

Malcolm Boyd, "A Play Called **Boy**"
(Reprinted from **Television Quarterly**)

13   Other Media [Wire Services, Films, Books], 132

A.J. Liebling, "The M.B.I." and
"Goodbye, M.B.I." (Reprinted from **The
Press** by A. J. Liebling)

14   Advertising
and Public Relations, 141

"No One Gets Hurt in This Rebellion, But
Dodge Auto Gets a Swinging Image"
(Reprinted from **Television** magazine)

PART FOUR

COVERAGE, 147

15 Coverage
    of Government, 149

Christopher Chandler, "**Sun-Times** Kills
Exposé of Swibel Renewal Deal"
(Reprinted from the **Chicago Journalism
Review**)

16 Coverage of Crimes
    and Demonstrations, 157

Nathan B. Blumberg, "A Study of the
'Orthodox' Press: The Reporting of
Dissent" (Reprinted from the **Montana
Journalism Review**)

17 Coverage of War
    and National Security, 164

Michael J. Arlen, "Morely Safer's
Vietnam" (Reprinted from **Living-Room
War** by Michael J. Arlen)

18 Coverage
    of Race, 170

Douglas Eldridge, "Reporting on Race"
(Reprinted from **Editor & Publisher**)

19 Coverage
    of Specialized News, 177

Peter Barnes, "The Wire Services in Latin
America" (Reprinted from **Nieman
Reports)**

Epilogue, 184

Preface

This book is designed primarily as a companion volume to the authors' **Media: An Introductory Analysis of American Mass Communications.** The chapter titles are identical with those of the text, and the introduction to each selection includes a brief summary of the text chapter.

We call this book a "casebook" instead of a "reader" because each selection offers a single example of a major problem or characteristic of the American mass media. Most readers are collections of essays; this one is a collection of examples. We hope these extended "cases" will help the student to understand the richness and complexity of the mass media. Whether or not this book is used in conjunction with the authors' text, we hope it will demonstrate the real world relevance of the theories and principles of mass communications.

We would like to extend our thanks to the authors and publishers of the selections that follow for permission to reprint their work. Most of these selections have never been anthologized; many are from relatively obscure sources. We take pleasure in making them public once again.

Peter M. Sandman
David M. Rubin
David B. Sachsman

Introduction

Communication is the process of transmitting a message from a source to an audience via a channel. It is also a sort of sharing process, an attempt to get the audience to share the views, attitudes, or information of the source—to share the message, in other words. We measure the success of a communication by the success of the sharing. The source may mumble his message, the channel may be overcome by static, the audience may fail to pay attention or to understand; in all these cases the communication has failed.

Mass communication is any communication aimed at an audience of more than one, usually through a machine. It differs from interpersonal communication in several important ways. First of all, the source of a mass communication does not know his audience personally and thus cannot gear his message to their individual quirks. Second, the mass-communication source is far less likely to get "feedback" from his audience as to whether or not they understand and agree. And third, mass-communication systems are a lot more complicated than interpersonal ones, with many different sources for the same message, many different audiences, and a complex organization serving as channel.

All three of these factors tend to lessen the effect of a mass communication on its audience. In fact, the mass media are likely to be most

1

effective when used in combination with interpersonal communication. Certain people, known as "opinion leaders," get their ideas on a given subject from the mass media. They then discuss the matter with their friends and neighbors, spreading the media's influence through the far more powerful channel of interpersonal communication. Though limited in their direct power, the media may thus have an enormous indirect impact.

The American system of mass communication is distinguished from other systems by three characteristics: pervasive influence, freedom of the press, and big-business journalism.

A fish could no more tell you what it is like to live out of water than an American could tell you what it is like to live without mass communication. By the time he enters kindergarten, the average American child has already been exposed to hundreds, perhaps thousands of hours of radio and television. He has attended dozens of movies and browsed through scores of children's books. He has cut pictures out of magazines and scowled at the newspaper in unconscious imitation of his daddy. All these experiences have taught him something. For most adults, meanwhile, the mass media constitute the only advanced education they will receive, and their number one recreational activity.

According to the American theory of government, the people control the government by electing officials to carry out their will. The role of the media is to give the people the information they need to intelligently instruct their officials. In order to do this, the media must be free from government control. Many have questioned whether or not the system works, whether or not the people are really well informed. But there is no doubt that the American mass media, by and large, are genuinely free from direct government interference.

Those who argue that freedom is no guarantee of public service often point to the big-business emphasis in modern American journalism. Like any business, the media are very concerned with stockholders, dividends, and profits. Like any business, they reflect a businessman's notion of what is good for the nation. And like any business, they do their best to gain and hold a monopoly.

This combination of factors makes the American mass media unique. Nowhere else is such a powerful social force so little controlled by government, so much controlled by self-interest.

The mass media in general, and the American mass media in particular, have four basic functions: to entertain, to inform, to influence, and to make money. Making money is, of course, the primary goal of the media, and they are overwhelmingly successful at it. To remain successful, the media must do a good job of influencing people—thus attracting advertisers. And they must do a good job of entertaining people—thus attracting audiences. The only function they can safely ignore is information, and ignore it they often do. Yet only the informing function of the media is essential to the survival of American democracy.

The selection that follows illustrates some of the interactions of these four functions.

ROBERT L. DUFFUS

To the Highest Bidder

I am an atom of moderate importance in the machine which turns out the Larkins City Gazette. The Larkins City Gazette is perhaps to be numbered among the first hundred daily newspapers of America, and Larkins City is of some significance to everyone who knows his America and of very great significance to those whose fortune it is to live there. Collectively we have played a part and are not to be ignored.

The masthead of the Gazette (how hard it is for me not to capitalize, too fondly, the first letter of that *The*!) carries the name of an owner and publisher and an editor. Those names have fluttered over many a battle of which we are not ashamed. But tomorrow the Gazette will be under a new flag. I have seen the proofs. The name of Herbert T. Perkins as well as my own modest "W. S. Lambert, Managing Editor," has been hauled down and where it once flew there flap alien and to my eyes hateful syllables.

Not that I love the name or person of Herbert T. Perkins, for to tell the truth I have rarely seen him and have only the remotest conception of his private virtues. But Herbert T. Perkins has stood for a kind of liberty. He had other interests than the Gazette, and by that miracle which happens now and then in journalism he did not use the Gazette to further those interests. In short he had only a passing and occasional concern for this property of his, so long as its circulation held up and its adverse balance did not strain his resources too severely. I think he took pride in being known as the owner of a newspaper. Possibly it satisfied a half sub-conscious literary aspiration. From our point of view the great merit of Mr. Perkins was that as a rule he left us alone. We ran the paper.

I shall not attempt to summarize the services of the Gazette in Larkins City. We began, humbly enough, by conducting campaigns for paved streets, fire-proof school buildings, and parks. From this field, in which we had the approval of almost all who called themselves good citizens, we were led into the more dangerous arcana of municipal corruption, and as we went higher and higher in our search for guilt the "good citizens" at first grew lukewarm and then turned savagely against us. But we built up a circulation which enabled us to defy our bankers and our advertisers and ventured further. Our crisis came when the employees of the street railways went on strike. We investigated their charges against the company, whose operations already smelled of corruption, and took their side. They won, in the end, a qualified victory. That was our supreme moment, although afterwards we elected a mayor and city council and cleaned up the town in earnest.

We were not always fighting, and we tried, indeed, to put the humorous and friendly aspects of town life into our paper. We believed in the old American traditions of democracy, and as far as we could we instilled them into our news and feature articles and editorials. Gradually we were aware of a following which believed in us, and which we could influence almost by a word. The rival daily lost circulation and would have lost advertising if advertising results had been the only ones the merchants sought. Often I have sat here in my office, late at night, and been conscious as I wrote of a friendly audience of hundreds, even thousands, of homely, steadfast Americans. I could almost see their faces. They came to our aid in our darkest hours. These, I sometimes thought, were Lincoln's people—the people who hated slavery. They were the best America had.

And somehow, for I never could believe that we deserved it, they trusted us. They trusted Herbert T. Perkins, and sent him letters that he never saw, under the impression that he wrote the paper as well as owned it. I think Herbert T. Perkins would have been puzzled by those letters, for allegiance to the people who wrote them was certainly far from his thoughts. He simply did not care about them, one way or the other. But he left us alone, and we went on making his name a magic one among readers he never so much as imagined.

This year Mr. Perkins, like others of his kind, has been pressed for money, and it may have been natural that he should realize upon the most outlying of his assets. I do not condemn him for selling the paper. Legally it was his property and we who trebled its circulation and multiplied its influence ten-fold were at all times his hired men. But the effect upon the institution we have erected was cataclysmic. For Mr. Perkins, in seeking a purchaser, turned to those who would pay most, and those who can afford to pay most are the very ones who do not want a newspaper like the Gazette in Larkins City. They have their own good reasons, on which I need not enlarge. They are a small minority in Larkins City, but they consider that the city is their property just as the insects in a cheese take a proprietary interest in their abiding place. I do not mean to be bitter, but this is the first image that occurs to me.

When the last edition has gone to press I shall roll down my sleeves, clean out my desk, put on my hat and coat and go home. I daresay I can find another job. Other men on the paper are not so hopeful. Some of them, who have children and own their own homes, will stay and help the new owner make the Gazette into a hateful mockery of its old self. I cannot endure that. At least, not having children, I will not.

I had an impulse to signalize the last day of the old ownership by a solemn funeral oration, in which I should warn our readers of what was to take place, but I thought better of it. The paper is not my property and it is perhaps not ethical to impair its money value—its goodwill, as the lawyers humorously call it—in this way.

The last proof has gone down. I have drawn my salary and that, with my pipe and a few books, is all I shall take with me when I step for the last time out of this building which contains so much of my life. What I cannot take will be destroyed. It will vanish like the old letters, proofs and newspapers I have been throwing on the floor around my desk for the janitor to sweep out. And the Gazette as we knew it, will vanish, too.

I remember a Civil War veteran who came into the office one day in the hottest of the traction fight. "I voted for Lincoln!" he told us, pounding the table with his old gnarled hand, "And I'll vote with you now. You boys are fighting Abe Lincoln's fight."

We laughed at him, or rather at ourselves, after he was gone; for we always made the pretense of being cynical. But we remembered him and he seemed the embodiment of throngs of those people who longed, pathetically, to see in the Gazette a pure and shining champion. I wonder what he will think. I wonder what all of them will think.

The paper is sold, safe enough, and the proper documents have changed hands. But as I pull my hat well down over my eyes and grope for the door it will be hard to escape the conviction that the new owner coming in tomorrow will take possession of something that does not belong to him.

PART ONE
DEVELOPMENT

1 Development

The history of journalism is to a large extent the history of the ways reporters have covered events. To illustrate this proposition, we have chosen an event that was extensively covered throughout U.S. history: the presidential nominating conventions of the two major political parties. From the Revolutionary period until well after the Civil War, the vast majority of American newspapers were deeply involved in national politics. Not only did they take a stand on all the big political issues, but their stands were nearly always based on loyal support of one of the two major parties. In 1844, for example, there were Whig newspapers and there were Democratic newspapers. Each paper printed only the news that favored its political champions, and each paper slanted that news heavily. Each was read only by those who agreed with its political convictions. One might almost say that the **purpose** of a newspaper in 1844 (as in 1780) was to carry the party line.

The "article" that follows is excerpted from the New York **Herald** of May 31, 1844. Though a front-page story, it is more extreme in its opinions (and in the way they are expressed) than a modern editorial. The Democrats had just nominated James K. Polk for President, and the **Herald**, a fervent supporter of Whig Henry Clay, was monumentally amused. It reported its amusement, and saved the details of the nomination itself for a "Postscript" lower down on the page.

THE DEMOCRATIC NOMINATIONS AT LAST—SINGULAR DENOUEMENT IN BALTIMORE

The city was astounded yesterday afternoon, on the arrival of the Railroad train from Philadelphia, with intelligence from Baltimore, that the regular Democratic Convention had unanimously nominated James K. Polk, of Tennessee for President, and Silas Wright, Jun. of New York, for Vice President. The complete and final defeat of Van Buren and Cass, has a most amusing and excruciating effect on the nervous system of the democracy.

The details of this interesting *denouement*, with the intelligence down to the latest hour on Wednesday evening, will be found annexed.

So at last Mr. Van Buren, the statesman, the politician, the "great magician," the man who walked so steadily in his "predecessor's footsteps" has at last got off the track, and is finally consigned to the philosophic shades of Lindenwald, on the banks of the beautiful Hudson, for the remainder of his natural life. This is a blow quite unexpected to his friends; but on looking calmly back on the last sixteen years, many will exclaim that it is what he had reason to expect. In the year 1823, Mr. Van Buren was the "master spirit," who entered into a movement that defeated the succession of Mr. Calhoun, after the first term of General Jackson. During the last three years Mr. Calhoun has returned the compliment, and has been the unseen power which conducted the movement that has defeated Mr. Van Buren's last and fondest hopes. . . .

Of the nomination of Mr. Polk we hardly know how to speak seriously. A more ridiculous, contemptible and forlorn candidate, was never put forth by any party. He has neither the vigor, respectability nor the elements of any reputation, even half so much as Captain Tyler and all the family, including the cracked head of old Wat Tyler. Mr. Polk is a sort of fourth or rather fortieth-rate lawyer and small politician in Tennessee, who by accident was once speaker of the House of Representatives. He was rejected even by his own state as governor—and now he comes forward as candidate of the great democracy of the United States. Oh! what a ridiculous *finale*. . . .

The singular result of all these laughable doings of the democracy in Baltimore, will be the election of Henry Clay, by a larger majority than ever was received by Jackson or Harrison. With Polk and Tyler in the field to divide the democracy, who, were they rolled into one person, would hardly make a man, Mr. Clay must get the State of New York with perfect ease. The same state of democratic disorganization will lead to the same results in other States. The presidential election may be said to be decided as soon as it opens. The democracy will be scattered to the four winds of heaven among their several candidates, and Clay will have only to *walk* *over the course.* The succession will soon become again the knotty point among politicians. We already see Daniel Webster in the field for the whig mantle in 1848, and John C. Calhoun for the democratic—all the other candidates of the latter camp have been disposed of in the general *melée* in Baltimore.

We annex the third and last day's business down to the latest hour. . . .

American newspapers in 1888 were still politically partisan, but they were much more interested in news. This is in part a reflection of the growing newspaper competition for unaligned readers. In part it reflects the diminishing partisanship of the American public. But the big reason for the change is neither of these. It is the telegraph, invented in 1844 and first extensively used during the Civil War. Because of the telegraph, a newspaper was actually able to report today's news today —or at least tomorrow. Readers and reporters both became preoccupied with speed as an end in itself. Editorial comment was secondary.

The stacked headlines and proud datelines of the two excerpts that follow clearly show a new interest in speed and "hard" news. Both are front-page articles. The first is from the San Francisco **Daily Examiner** of June 7, 1888; the second is from the New York **Tribune** of the same date. Both report the nomination of Democrat Grover Cleveland.

In comparison with the 1844 story, these are models of objectivity. Outright political opinion is completely missing. What was a factual "Postscript" in 1844 is now the whole story. But by modern standards these are still strange articles. They are organized, not in order of importance, but in chronological order, taking several thousand words to get to the details of the nomination itself. Moreover, both stories are clearly biased in their choice of words and images. It is not difficult to figure out that the **Examiner** supported Cleveland, whereas the **Tribune** opposed him.

HIS REWARD

Grover Cleveland Renominated for President

Not an Opposing Voice

Dougherty's Magnificent Eulogy of Democracy's Leader

His Hearers Furious with Joy

A Scene Scarcely Ever Before Paralleled

ADJOURNED UNTIL TODAY

[Special to the EXAMINER]

ST. LOUIS, June 6.—When the convention assembled this morning there were abundant evidences that a vast contingent of the gallant Democracy of the country had passed a wild night. There was a tired and thoughtful look upon the faces of the multitude—a look suggesting the need of bromide and Apollinaris water.

When the delegates began to assemble in their places, Virginia anticipated California and hoisted a red bandana. Nevada and West Virginia followed. When Pennsylvania threw up a bandana over its standard there was a general round of applause. The first Californian who arrived at the seat of his delegation hurriedly drew his bandana from his pocket and knotted it tightly about the top of his California staff.

Georgia, which entered next, did not applaud the Californians. Among them were some of the friends of ex-Minister Henry Jackson, concerning whom the wrathful Old Roman made an uncomplimentary remark. They hung up a small American flag from their banneret.

The Indiana delegation hung up a black silk hat, round which was wound a gray silk handkerchief.

Nebraska surprised the Gray men by hanging up a gray tile, but it developed that this was a Cleveland and not a Gray hat.

Tennessee also hung up the black hat. These indications did not, however, excite much attention among the delegates.

When at precisely 10:20 the electrical voice of Chairman White rang through the edifice its effect was at once seen and inspired the faces of the weary with that vim and energy so displayed yesterday.

Getting down to work again Mr. White cudgled the desk with a mighty club and in that great voice of his commanded the delegates to take their seats.

When White commands it is customary to obey. In five minutes dead silence reigned in the huge hall.

Then Mr. White roared out the name of the Rev. Mr. Green, who folded his hands and lifted his voice in prayer. . . .

It was seen at once it was time for the Cleveland idea to assert itself, and he wanted the convention to go into nomination for President and Vice-President, amid roars that shook the glazed roof of the great nave. This was carried, and in five minutes more a tall, gray side-whiskered man was seen mounting the steps, and when the Chairman announced the name of Daniel Dougherty of New York there was a tremendous outburst, as everybody knew what he was there for. Mr. Dougherty looks like Mr. Gladstone.

A Consummate Orator

Many people thought that in that great hall not a sound from his old frame could be heard, but they doubtless did not know the orator.

Dougherty is a marvel and wonder in the science of oratory. His voice is a dream of melody, his gesticulation the very poetry of motion. As he stepped forward and uttered his first phrase—just one that he projected on a single breath to attract the attention of his hearers—he threw back his head like a great elk tossing back his antlers; he let fall his right arm in a magnificent side sweep and then paused. As the words shot out there was such a musical ring to them, such a pleas-

ant change from the metallic sound of the reading clerk's and the previous speakers, that it seemed as if the dulcet tones of a flute had fallen upon ears weary with the hammering of iron. It was the range and music of an orator.

As the first words rose above the State banners and passed on and over the alternates till they reached the farthest corner, one thought of Gladstone and his bell-like voice, of Cicero in the Forum, of Demosthenes teaching his voice the murmur of the Grecian waves.

Thousands of those who were in the convention for the first time were stilled into silence. Even California neglected its bandanas. Then, as the clear-cut sentences began to be appreciated and the orator seemed to be reaching his great point, the bustle of expectancy began and soon burst its bonds.

The Climax

Mr. Dougherty gave only a note of warning. Stopping just one instant, he raised the two quivering hands far above his head and kept them there, and with a thrilling invocation to heaven, and with passionate tones, said: "I shall present a name which is entwined in the hearts of the people. It is the name of 'Grover.——'"

He got no further. The yells which met his words seemed to explode, to break with one wild, harmonious, uncontrollable, spontaneous impulse from every throat in the hall. It came like the first burst of a cyclone, with the power that can only be described as awful.

The scene which followed

beggars description. With that yell every man, and woman, too, was on foot. The men acted like lunatics. They sprang to their chairs, hats flew into the air, fans and papers were hurled across the hall.

The main floor, every seat of which had been filled when the nomination speech began, looked like a field of waving hats, canes and handkerchiefs, thick as a field of corn.

Seemed to Have Gone Crazy

The assemblage thrilled with enthusiasm and the opening yell grew into a continuous roar, which never diminished or ceased, but seemed to increase in swelling volume of sound until the noise was hurtful to the ear.

The New Yorkers were frantic. One man grabbed the standard of the State and waved it wildly. The example was caught up by other delegations and the standards of all the States were soon waving above the hats and handkerchiefs.

English of California got a pole twenty feet long and swung the red bandana above all the banners. The New Yorkers stood on their seats and waved everything they could find. Umbrellas were hoisted on the floor and the standards with their gay colors went clear to the roof. Pasteboard eagles were lifted from their fastenings and their wings made to flap.

The shouts of delegates passed in an instant through the alternates and the spectators around them. The sound was caught up by the galleries and swept around them. The men in the Vice-Presidents' box were on their feet, shouting themselves hoarse and vying with the young Democracy in exertion.

When there was the slightest sign of the tremendous applause ceasing some club, or section of the hall, would renew it with a scream that inspired the entire assemblage again.

A Lull Suggested

In mercy to the people the Chairman at length interposed, and after repeated efforts directed their attention to a tall Kentuckian who stood beside him. This gentleman, Delegate Mackenzie, was to second the nomination of Cleveland and aroused the convention to a renewed outburst almost at the first word, by declaring that there was but one Democrat in the country more popular than Cleveland—the queenly woman he has made his wife.

Again the convention was in an uproar when the speaker gave a brand new title to the leader of the Republicans, "The Florentine Mosaic from Maine."

Mr. Mackenzie moved now to suspend the rules and make the nomination of Cleveland absolutely unanimous.

But everybody wished to join in seconding the nomination of Cleveland, and everybody was given a chance. Then the thing was done with one loud-resounding hurrah. . . .

CLEVELAND NOMINATED

A VOTE BY STATES FOUND UNNECESSARY

THE CONVENTION TAKES MOST OF ITS CHEERING IN ONE DOSE—THE FRIENDS OF THURMAN OUTGENERALLED—AN ADJOURNMENT WHICH GAVE HOPE TO GRAY'S SUPPORTERS

[BY TELEGRAPH
TO THE TRIBUNE]

St. Louis, June 6.—Mr. Cleveland was renominated today by acclamation. The convention succeeded in accomplishing this much of the task laid out for it in Washington. It was not the intention to make either nomination, apparently, until after the platform had been adopted, but the convention got into the humor for doing something, being weary of waiting on the Committee on Resolutions, and so, having nothing better to do, in more senses than one, it nominated Mr. Cleveland. When it became known, however, that the Committee on Resolutions could not possibly report before tomorrow morning, a portion of the convention, made up largely of friends of Governor Gray, asked to have the nomination of a candidate for Vice-President postponed until after the platform had been disposed of, and this was done. When the convention came together an hour later the hall was even more crowded, if possible, than it had been yesterday. Every part of the space was packed with people. The heat was great, and there was a steady flutter of thousands of fans. Hundreds of men had their coats off among the spectators.

The upper gallery was lined all along the front with men in their shirt sleeves. The first business was to receive the report of the Committee on Credentials, which disposed of the only contest, that in Dakota, by seating the Administration delegation, that of Governor Church, whom President Cleveland transplanted from Jamaica, Long Island, to that far off Territory.

Congressman Collins Warmly Received

The report of the Committee on Permanent Organization presented as permanent chairman Patrick A. Collins, of Massachusetts, who was warmly welcomed, not only for himself, but also undoubtedly for the class of voters whom this selection was intended to flatter. Mr. Collins showed an erect, stalwart figure, and a face indicative both of resolution and good humor. His voice is pleasing, but far from being as effective for convention purposes as the shriller tones of Mr. White, temporary chairman. To most of Mr. Collins's audience, his address must have been entirely inaudible, but it was received by the delegates with every sign of interest, although it was read from manuscript. It was frequently applauded. At his first mention of Cleveland there was a spurt of a cheer, and when he paid his tribute to the Mugwumps, to whom he said the Democratic party owed a debt of gratitude, there were a few isolated hand-claps. His elaborate tribute to the President, in concluding, was once or twice interrupted with cheers, and there was a straggling shout at the close. . . .

The Committee on Resolutions being unable to report, W. N. Hensel, chairman of the Pennsylvania delegation, moved that the roll be called for the presentation of candidates, it being understood that no vote should be taken until the platform had been disposed of. This was received with great cheering in the galleries, where they wanted to see the fun begin. The motion was carried, and the roll-call began. Alabama surrendered its right, when its name was called, to the State of New-York. Cheering broke out at this, which grew into a roar as Daniel Dougherty rose amid the New-York delegation and be-

gan to make his way toward the stage. His colleagues in the New-York delegation rose in a body, headed by the indefatigable Roswell P. Flower, and cheered him. Many other delegates sprang to their feet and joined in the applause. Mr. Dougherty is a stately gentleman of the old school, with a courtly bearing, handsome silver sidewhiskers, and that air of intense respectability, that is nowhere found in such perfection as in the climate of Philadelphia, from which he recently emigrated. There was a little of the tragedian's swinging stride in Mr. Dougherty's walk, as he advanced toward the platform. The scene was animated, if Mr. Dougherty was not. The Convention was on its feet cheering. Red bandannas were waving everywhere. Ladies' white handkerchiefs were fluttering, and fans were wildly brandished above their owners' heads. Mr. Dougherty's oratory was seen to be of the old school also, and did not greatly move the Convention. There was more manner in it than matter, but he was liberally applauded, and when he closed by pronouncing the name of Grover Cleveland, which he had kept in reserve for a climax, the storm of cheering burst out. . . .

From 1888 to 1928, newspaper circulation in the United States increased more than tenfold. Immigration, urbanization, and education were responsible for the new readers. The effect on the media was overwhelming.

For one thing, newspapers were forced to cut the excess verbiage out of their styles. Flowery writing was fine for the upper-class audience of the nineteenth century, but the new audience of the twentieth had neither the time nor the inclination (nor the skill) to wade through mountains of prose in search of facts. For the same reason, the leisurely hronological structure of the 1800s had to be abandoned. Readers wanted the most important news first, and newspapers learned to give it o them in that order.

Along with these trends developed the "cult of objectivity." The wire services helped to point the way. In an effort to please publishers with all sorts of viewpoints, AP, UP, and INS wrote without any viewpoint. The wire story—an assortment of "raw facts" roughly in order of mportance—became the epitome of good newspaper journalism. Interpretation and opinion were exiled to the editorial page.

The **New York Times** was the foremost expression of this universal deal. The excerpt that follows is from the front page of the **Times** of June 15, 1928. It reports the nomination of Republican Herbert Hoover. The **Times** opposed Hoover—but it is impossible to tell this from the story.

HOOVER NAMED ON FIRST BALLOT BY 837; LOWDEN SECOND WITH 74; CURTIS GETS 64; FARMERS SQUELCHED ON FLOOR, 807 TO 277

QUICK VICTORY FOR HOOVER

His Nomination Follows a Night of Long and Fervid Oratory

LOWDEN WITHDRAWS NAME

Acts at Last Minute as Protest Over Farm Declaration He Regards as Inadequate

---

BUT HE LEADS THE RIVALS

Coolidge Gets 17 Votes, Hughes 1, Dawes 4, Watson 45 and Norris 24

By RICHARD V. OULAHAN

Special to The New York Times
    KANSAS CITY, June 14.—
Herbert Hoover of California
was nominated for President of

the United States by the Republican National Convention at 11:20 o'clock tonight (1:20 o'clock Friday morning, New York Daylight Saving Time).

    The nomination came to Mr.

Hoover on the first ballot. He received 837 votes.

The other 200-odd represented in the convention went to the various contenders for the nomination and to some whose names had not been presented when nominating speeches were made at a session that began at 7 o'clock this evening and ended just after Mr. Hoover's victory was announced officially.

The vote in detail was as follows:

Hoover	837
Lowden	74
Curtis	64
Watson	45
Norris	24
Goff	18
Coolidge	17
Dawes	4
Hughes	1
Not Voting	5
Total	1,089

The convention adjourned until noon tomorrow, when it will devote itself to its concluding duty of choosing a candidate for Vice President.

Seeks Vice Presidency Solution

When the convention adjourned, various groups of leading Republicans went into conference in the hope of being able to adjust the conflicting and embarrassing Vice Presidential situation before the convention convened for its final session.

Late tonight the chief conference was in progress in the headquarters of Secretary Mellon in the Hotel Muelhbach. Prior to the time the conferees met the understanding prevailed that the principal contest over Vice Presidential honors

had narrowed down to a choice between Senator Moses of New Hampshire and Senator Deneen of Illinois, with Deneen reluctant to have his name presented to the convention, and Moses seemingly having a shade the better of it.

A new name was brought into the situation in that of former Governor Channing Cox of Massachusetts, who was proposed on the ground that his candidacy on the Hoover ticket may save his State from going Democratic in the Presidential elections. The Pennsylvania delegation strongly urged that he be selected for second place on the national ticket.

Convention Quiet at Climax

That Hoover would be chosen to lead the party in this year's Presidential campaign had been certain for days. The honor came to him at a time when the convention, tired out after two long sessions and fatigued by the cheering that marked tonight's proceedings, was not in a mood for a demonstration.

There was no outburst of enthusiasm such as might have been expected when victory perched itself at last on the Hoover banner. A cheer or two went up and then the convention was quiet while delegates from three States that had opposed Hoover's candidacy—Kansas, Oklahoma and West Virginia—moved that the nomination be made unanimous.

Senator Moses, the presiding officer, called for a viva voce expression. There was a great chorus of "aye." When he called for the nays, delegates from Wisconsin shouted a loud "no." But Moses declared that the motion to make the nomination unanimous had been carried and he read to the convention a telegram which he said had already been sent to Secretary Hoover notifying him of his nomination and congratulating him in the convention's name. . . .

Hard on the heels of Hoover's election came the Great Depression of the 1930s. Suddenly the world seemed incredibly complicated, and "raw facts" proved inadequate for the job of explaining it. When the United States went off the gold standard in 1933, President Roosevelt sent a group of White House economic advisers over to the pressroom to help reporters understand the meaning of the move. The reporters were grateful, and interpretive news articles soon became commonplace.

The growth of broadcasting contributed to the trend. Unlike the printing press, the vacuum tube requires no typesetters and no delivery boys. Radio and television can have a story on the air minutes after the event; newspapers take hours. By the end of the 1930s it was obvious to editors that speed was no longer a reasonable goal for newspapers. They might still serve the public by supplying the details of the news, or the significance of the news—but broadcasters were bound to get there first with the news itself.

When Richard Nixon was nominated by the Republican party in 1968, two of the three networks carried the convention live. The next morning (August 8), the Los Angeles **Times** ran two front-page articles on the nomination. One story reported the event itself; the other offered background material. Both were essentially objective, but both were highly interpretive. From the two excerpts that follow, you cannot tell that the **Times** supported Nixon in the election. But you can tell a great deal about the man and his party that no newspaper would have seen fit to report in 1928.

NIXON NOMINATED ON FIRST BALLOT

TALLIES 692; PUT OVER TOP BY WISCONSIN

BY ROBERT J. DONOVAN

Times Washington Bureau Chief

MIAMI BEACH—Richard M. Nixon was nominated for President by the Republicans on the first ballot early today and, with deafening cheers, was sent forth into one of the most momentous campaigns in American history.

In a great political comeback from disastrous election defeats in 1960 and 1962, the former Vice President crushed the challenges of Govs. Reagan of California and Nelson A. Rockefeller of New York and thus probably kept the party from swerving either to the right or left.

Wisconsin put him over the top at the Republican National Convention at 1:50 a.m. EDT, after he had swept the South and had picked up large blocs of votes in the border states, the Midwest, the Rocky Mountain region and the Pacific Northwest.

With 667 votes needed for victory the outcome of the roll call was:

Nixon	692
Rockefeller	277
Reagan	182

The Nixon nomination—later made unanimous at Reagan's request—merely strengthens the prospect that Vice President Humphrey will be nominated by the Democratic Party in Chicago three weeks hence. Whereas Democrats believe that Humphrey has a fighting chance at least against Nixon, the nomination of Rockefeller might have frightened them into a stampede to Sen. Eugene J. McCarthy (D-Minn.).

Exerting Pressure on Nixon

A critical decision lies ahead of the 55-year-old Nixon and the convention today in the selection of a vice presidential nominee.

Southern conservatives, led by Sen. Strom Thurmond of South Carolina, are exerting heavy pressure on Nixon not to choose a liberal. Sen. Mark O. Hatfield of Oregon, a moderate, is considered a strong possibility. Others being mentioned are Sens. Charles H. Percy of Illinois and Howard Baker Jr. of Tennessee, son-in-law of Sen. Everett M. Dirksen of Illinois.

Because Nixon is caught in a potentially damaging squeeze between Southern conservatives and big-city liberals, his choice of a running mate is likely to be a symbol that will affect his campaign in one way or another.

Acceptance Speech Tonight

After his victory Nixon, who will deliver his acceptance speech to the convention tonight, quickly predicted that the Democratic Party would be badly split in the campaign.

Nixon said he won the nomination "without having to pay any price or make any deals."

The Republican Party, including the vanquished Rockefeller and Reagan, quickly closed ranks around the nominee and pledged support in the campaign ahead.

Smiling as brightly as if he had won, Reagan strode to the podium soon after the roll call and declared that the Democrats must be tossed out in November. Then he offered resolution that the roll call be made unanimous, and the convention roared its approval.

Rockefeller telephoned his congratulations, promised his support and said in a press conference, "I wish him all the success in winning the election in November." . . .

NIXON COMEBACK HAD ITS
START IN ASHES OF 1964
GOP DEBACLE

Took Shape When He Helped Party
Rebound in 1966 to Win 47 Seats in
House, 3 in Senate and 8 Governorships

BY DON IRWIN
Times Staff Writer

MIAMI BEACH—Richard M. Nixon's long quest for the second chance at the Presidency he won Wednesday grew paradoxically from the GOP debacle of 1964.

The dream that began four years ago took concrete form when the Republicans—with Nixon's vigorous aid—bounced back in 1966 to win 47 seats in the House, three in the Senate and eight governorships.

With the vest pocket staff he had assembled for his volunteer role in that campaign, Nixon spent election night, Tuesday, Nov. 8, 1966, watching returns in a Manhattan hotel room. He left at midnight for his 5th Ave. apartment but telephoned the room at 2:30 a.m. for a rundown.

Savors Results in Detail

State by state, victory by victory, he savored the results in detail.

"We've beaten hell out of them and we're going to kill them in '68," was his reaction. To his aides it meant: "Let's go."

It was a summons to an endeavor at once daring and methodically professional, that has lifted Nixon from the limbo of an also-ran back to the national standard-bearer's role at which he failed in 1960.

Critics charge that Nixon's second try is rooted only in unfulfilled ambition. But Nixon's version, presented Wednesday at a convention news conference, is that he is running because "this is the time, I think, when the man and the moment in history come together."

"I have always felt that a man cannot seek the Presidency and get it simply because he wants it," Nixon said. "I think that he can seek the Presidency and obtain it only when the Presidency requires what he may have to offer."

Nixon, whose critics call him a "plastic man" who trims his views to events, contended that any intelligent man changes his approaches as facts change. Such a man is not an opportunist, he said, but "a pragmatist, a realist."

To win the nomination, Nixon invested 18 months of quiet effort and half a year of public campaigning. He did his best to show himself as a man able at once to unify his party and to wage and win campaigns. His chosen instrument was the 1968 GOP primaries. . . .

The final excerpt in this chapter was also written in 1968 and als reports the nomination of Richard Nixon. It appeared not in a news paper but in **Harper's** magazine, and later in book form. Its author i Norman Mailer—one of the foremost exponents of the "New Journal ism."

The New Journalism is interpretive reporting taken one step further The author not only presents the background of events, but also make clear his own views—through adjectives and images, and sometime through explicit statements of opinion. He pays little attention to th traditional structure of a news story, but rather reports actions in the order in which they happened. His writing is not as spare as typical newspaper writing; instead, it is studded with personal, colorful, and admittedly biased "word pictures."

If this sounds like our description of the New York **Herald** of 1844 it is no accident. Norman Mailer's vast personal following would have shocked the anonymous editors of 1844. But in essence the New Jour nalism is not new. It has simply been in hiding for the last hundred odd years. The interesting question is this: Will it return to newspaper in the next decade or two, or will it remain strictly the province of opinion magazines and books?

NORMAN MAILER

Miami and the Siege of Chicago

On Wednesday night Alabama ceded to California, and Reagan was first to be in nomination. Ivy Baker Priest made the speech, Ivy Baker Priest Stevens was her name now, a handsome woman who had been Treasurer of the United States in Eisenhower's cabinet, and then an assistant to Reagan. She had a dual personality. She was a wretched speaker with the parched nasal mean stingy acid driving tones of a typical Republican lady speaker: "A man who will confront the radicals on our campuses

New York: The World Publishing Company, Signet Books, pp. 66–70. Reprinted by permission of The World Publishing Company from *Miami and the Siege of Chicago* by Norman Mailer. Copyright © 1968 by Norman Mailer.

nd the looters on our streets and say, 'The laws will be obeyed.'" It as a relief when her nasalities began to drive up the hill and one knew e mention of Reagan's name was near. "A man to match our moun-ins and our plains, a man steeped in the glorious traditions of the past, man with a vision of the unlimited possibilities of a new era. Yes, Destiny has found the man." A minute later she was done, and a fairly rge demonstration went to work. It was to prove milder and less im-ressive than the Rockefeller and Nixon break-outs, but it was at least otable for a sight of the opposite side of the lady's personality. She ow looked confident, enthusiastic, round, sexy, warm, and gloriously ital, the best blond housemother you could ever see, waving the fra-ernity boys around the bend as they sang "Dixie" and "California, Here Come," clapping her hands in absolute delight at signs like "I'm gone n Ron," as if that were absolutely the most attractive thing she'd ever een, then jazzed it like a cheerleader beating her palms and smiling, miling at the sight of each new but familiar crew-cut face who had got-en up to whoop and toot it through the aisles for Ronnie. There were ive cages of balloons overhead, and Reagan got one of them, the bal-oons came down in a fast cascade—each one blessed with a drop of vater within so as to tend to plummet rather than tend to float—and they ame down almost as fast as foam rubber pillows and were detonated vith lighted cigarettes and stomping feet thus immediately that a string f firecrackers could have gone off.

When that was done, a monumental sense of tedium overtook the ight. Hickel of Alaska and Winthrop Rockefeller of Arkansas were put n as favorite sons, the latter with two seconding speeches and an eight-ninute demonstration—he was conceivably giving nothing to his brother -Romney used all of forty minutes, Nelson Rockefeller's band boosting is demonstration as Romney troops were later to boost Rockefeller's. Senator Carlson of Kansas was named as favorite son, then Hiram Fong f Hawaii. It was after nine before Governor Shafer of Pennsylvania tood up to put Nelson Rockefeller on the lists. More than two and a alf hours had elapsed between the end of Reagan's presentation and the eginning of Rocky's. Reporters had left the convention hall, and were uddled backstage in places like the Railroad Lounge where free sand-viches and beer were available, and everybody was concerned with the nost attractive proposition of the night—that if they were all to go to heir hotels, check out, and catch a plane, they could be at their homes before nominations were done and balloting had begun. They could vatch it on television, which was the real gloom of the occasion. The convention had demonstrated that no reporter could keep up any longer vith the event unless checking in periodically with the tube; the politi-cians, themselves, rushed forward to TV men, and shouldered note-pads

aside. During this lull, therefore, one bitter reporter, a big heavy South
ern boy with horn-rimmed glasses, delivered the remark of the evening
Sipping beer and glumly munching his sandwich (which held an inch o
paper-dry turkey) he said, "Yessir, the only thing which could liven uj
this convention is if Ike was to croak tonight." So the respect journalists
had been obliged to pay over the years could be tolerated now only by
the flensing knives of the club.

Shafer put Rockefeller in ". . . because he is in tune. The people
young and old, rich and poor, black and white, have responded to him
He has never lost an election. . . . Ladies and gentlemen, we should
nominate Nelson Rockefeller because he is the Republican who can most
surely win. . . ." It was an inept speech—Rocky's name was mentioned
seven times before the signal was given to the delegates, and tension was
dissipated. It didn't matter. Everyone knew that Rockefeller would
have an enormous demonstration and that it would not matter. The day
when demonstrations could turn a convention were gone. The demonstrators knew they would be chided in newspaper editorials the following
day, and therefore were sheepish in the very middle of their stomping
and their jigging. Soon they would hold conventions in TV studios.

Then came Spiro Agnew for Nixon. If he had not been selected for
Vice President next day, his speech would have gone unnoticed and
unremarked—"It is my privilege to place in nomination for the office o
President of the United States the one man whom history has so clearly
thrust forward, the one whom all America will recognize as a man whose
time has come, the man for 1968, the Honorable. . . ."

Nixon's demonstration was about equal to Rockefeller's. Hordes of
noise, two cages of balloons, machine-gun drumfire as they went out—no
lift in the audience, no real lift. Nothing this night could begin to recall
that sense of barbarians about a campfire and the ecstasy of going to
war which Barry Goldwater had aroused in '64.

Still the demonstrations gave another image of the three candidacies:
Reagan's men had straight hair cropped short, soldiers and state troopers
for Ronnie; so far as Republicans were swingers, so swingers marched
with Rocky; and for Nixon—the mood on the floor was like the revel in
the main office of a corporation when the Christmas Party is high.

More nominations. Harold Stassen for the seventh time. Senator
Case of New Jersey, Governor Rhodes of Ohio, Senator Thurmond who
immediately withdrew for Nixon. At 1:07 A.M., eight hours and seven
minutes after the convention had opened for nomination, it was closed,
and over the floor rested the knowledge that nothing had happened tonight. It had been Nixon on the first ballot from the beginning, and it
was Nixon at the end. By the time Alabama, the first state, voted, 14 for
Nixon, 12 for Reagan, the next to last doubt was dispelled, for *The New*

York Times on Sunday had estimated only 9 solid for Nixon. When Florida came in with 32 out of 34, and Georgia with 21 where only 14 had seemed likely a few days before, there was no need to worry the issue. Wisconsin with 30 votes for Nixon carried it over—the total was 692. The rest had gone: Rockefeller 277, Reagan 182, Rhodes 55, Romney 50, Case 22, Carlson 20, W. Rockefeller 18, Fong 14, Stassen 2, Lindsay 1.

Filing out of the hall, there was the opportunity to see Nixon on television. Where in 1960 he had said, "All I am I owe to my mother and father, my family and my church . . ." he was considerably more of the professional strategist tonight as he spoke of his efforts to win the nomination while unifying the party. "You see," he said to the cameras, "the beauty of our contest this year was that we won the nomination in a way designed to win the election. We didn't make the mistake of breaking up the California delegation or breaking up the Ohio delegation or raiding the Michigan delegation. And in the State of New York also we respected the Rockefeller position, being the candidate for New York. And I think this will pay off in November. We're going to have a united party. Sure we've had a real fight . . . but we have won it in a way that we're going into the final campaign united." He was lucid, he was convincing, he said he felt perfectly "free" to choose his Vice President. "I won the nomination without having to pay any price, making any deal with any candidate or any individuals representing a candidate. . . . I [will] meet with delegates from all over the country . . . Southern delegates, the Northern delegates, the Midwestern delegates and the Western delegates. But I will make the decision based on my best judgment as to the man that can work best with me, and that will, I think perhaps, if he ever has to do that, serve as President of the United States."

In the old days, he had got his name as Tricky Dick because he gave one impression and acted upon another—later when his language was examined, one could not call him a liar. So he had literally not made any deal with any candidate, but he was stretching the subtle rubber of his own credibility when he claimed he would not have to pay any price. The rest of the night at the Miami Hilton would belong to the South.

PART TWO
RESPONSIBILITY

2 Self-Control

Sociologists claim that one of the defining characteristics of a "profession" is the existence of a formal code of ethics. If so, then journalism is not a profession. Doctors and lawyers are told by their colleagues precisely what is ethical and what is not, and if they violate the code they may be expelled from the profession. But a reporter must set his own ethical standards. At most he may be fired by his publisher, not by his fellow reporters.

Not that the mass media are without their formal codes. Almost every medium has one, including even the Comics Magazine Association of America. But these codes are little more than collections of platitudes, with few specific provisions and no means of enforcement.

Consider, for example, the Canons of Journalism of the American Society of Newspaper Editors. Canon One, "Responsibility," reads as follows:

> The right of a newspaper to attract and hold readers is restricted by nothing but considerations of public welfare. The use a newspaper makes of the share of public attention it gains serves to determine its sense of responsibility, which it shares with every member of its staff. A journalist who uses his power for any selfish or otherwise unworthy purpose is faithless to a high trust.

That is not a preamble. It is the entire "Responsibility" section. Journalism offers few ethical solutions, but it is rife with ethical problems. The following are typical: When, if ever, is it more important to respect the privacy of a news source than to get the story? Should a reporter be permitted to take personal advantage of inside information (such as a stock-market tip)? Should reporters be allowed to moonlight as press agents or public-relations men? When is it acceptable for a newsman to accept a gift or a junket from a source? Is it ethical for a reporter to pay a source for an exclusive interview? What about pretending not to be a reporter in order to get the story?

There are no easy answers to any of these questions. And journalists in search of the hard answers must find them on their own. The formal media codes will not help.

One of the most common ethical problems in journalism is experienced by the reporter who gets involved in his story as something other than an observer. Political correspondents are especially prone to this malady. A newsman assigned to cover, say, the Pentagon spends many hours a day in the company of military personnel. He makes friends, builds alliances, and after a year or two he starts thinking like a general. Inevitably he develops opinions on the main policy issues confronting the military. He may even serve as an informal adviser and part-time press secretary for his favorite news source. All these activities have an influence on the kinds of articles he writes and the way he writes them.

In the power-charged atmosphere of Washington politics, it takes a very strong-willed reporter (or a very lazy one) to remain a strictly neutral observer. Most get involved in behind-the-scenes politicking of one sort or another. Often they do a tremendous amount of good in the process—but their neutrality as reporters is compromised nonetheless.

The selection that follows reports a typical case—that of Sanford Watzman of the Cleveland **Plain Dealer**. Most readers will agree that Watzman's opposition to overcharging on defense contracts was justified. The series of articles he wrote on the subject was admirable. But Watzman didn't just write the series; he used it to force a bill through Congress, becoming a part-time Congressman as well as a reporter. The question is not whether the results Watzman achieved were desirable. The question is whether a reporter should ever forfeit his neutrality and become an activist. It is an open question.

CAPITAL NEWSMEN OFTEN PLAY A ROLE IN CREATING THE EVENTS THEY COVER

By NOEL EPSTEIN

WASHINGTON—One afternoon last spring, Sanford (Whitey) Watzman, a reporter for the Cleveland Plain Dealer, was sitting in the House press gallery feeling rather pleased. "Nobody noticed," he said, "but they passed my bill today."

It wasn't an idle boast. For more than a year, Whitey Watzman, reporter, had been doubling as Whitey Watzman, Congressional strategist; he had played a significant behind-the-scenes role in winning House adoption of a measure authorizing the Pentagon to check contractors' books for possible overcharges on about $5 billion a year of defense work not put up for competitive bidding.

Indeed, it was Whitey Watzman who conceived of the legislation. It was Whitey Watzman who privately urged members of Congress to introduce it. It was Whitey Watzman who provided prompting to help keep it moving. It was, in many respects, Whitey Watzman's bill. And, standing a good chance of final passage by the Senate before adjournment this fall, it could become Whitey Watzman's Law.

The fact is that the influential Washington press corps' powers extend considerably beyond reporting and interpreting the news unfolding in the capital. Unknown to their readers, newsmen here, and particularly investigative reporters, sometimes are the prime promoters or offstage prompters in the Congressional hearings, legislative battles and other events they are chronicling, theoretically with detachment. This practice of "not only getting it from the horse's mouth but being inside his mouth" is "almost a way of life for many columnists and some reporters here," says Laurence Stern, an assistant managing editor of the Washington Post.

Assuring Publicity

Busy members of Congress generally welcome such newsmen's assistance, and for good reason. It often supplies them with fresh, ready-made issues to seize upon and, perhaps more important, it almost guarantees that their efforts will receive prominent attention in the reporter's publication—which is often a newspaper published in the officeholder's home territory.

For reporters, the double role can gain wider recognition for news stories they initiate or feel strongly about, while also promoting causes they believe to be in the public interest. (Congressional press gallery rules forbid any lobbying by the 1,050 member correspondents from the daily press and the

From *The Wall Street Journal*, 79, no. 51 (September 11, 1968), 1, 23. Used by permission. Copyright © 1968 by *The Wall Street Journal*.

400 radio and television and 500 periodical representatives, but this bar is aimed mainly at preventing legislative pressure work by reporters for special interests and for profit.)

Charles Nicodemus of the Chicago Daily News is among those who have climbed "inside the horse's mouth," helping to draft speech material and then reporting the ideas as those of the officeholder he aided. He played just such a duet with Republican Rep. Paul Findley of home-state Illinois during the 1967 dispute over the Government-authorized sale of M-16 rifles to Singapore while the weapons were in short supply for Vietnam troops—a story Mr. Nicodemus uncovered.

A Congressman Sounds Off

"When I first got word of what was cooking, I wanted someone to raise hell in public about it," he says. "So I got in touch with Findley, who I had worked with before. . . . I fed him stuff and he sounded off about it, and he asked the State Department or Defense about other things." Mr. Nicodemus won a distinguished service award from Sigma Delta Chi, the professional journalism society, for these and related stories.

Currently back in Chicago as the News' political editor, Mr. Nicodemus remarks that he is "the first to say there are real problems involved" in playing such dual roles. But he adds: "You come to feel that when you're dealing with a crucial subject like this, where guys' lives are involved, someone ought to be doing something about it. And if a reporter is the only one around with the time or inclination, he'd better well do it."

Some other Washington reporters, like Pulitzer Prize-winner Clark Mollenhoff of the Des Moines Register and the Minneapolis Tribune, expend much effort trying to promote Congressional investigations. Mr. Mollenhoff says he has been attempting to interest "countless Senators and Congressmen" in a broad inquiry into what he considers the questionable way North American Aviation Inc. received major contracts for the Apollo moon-landing program. In May and June of 1967, Mr. Mollenhoff wrote several articles on the subject, tied to the Senate hearings on the Apollo fire that killed three astronauts, but the issue has been dormant since.

"I wish I could stir five times as much interest," he says. "But the committees are touchy about getting into it. They work closely with the agencies they supervise, and too often they aren't the policemen they're supposed to be."

A Potential Danger

A somewhat comparable conflict of interest, however, is one of the dangers critics see in reporters' close collaboration with officeholders they cover. The Washington Post's Mr. Stern, for one, says "the integrity of their stories and their ability to look at an official impartially become compromised." (Dual-role practitioners, however, maintain that they would criticize in print any of the Republicans or Democrats they deal with, if criticism were due.)

Doubters also complain that voters may get a distorted impression when a cooperating officeholder receives heavy press attention—since his outpourings really are partly the reporter's ideas. They suggest that the reporter might take a leave of absence or work full-time for the legislator if he feels that strongly about an issue.

But others, like Los Angeles Times correspondent Robert Jackson, tend to applaud the newsman who also dons the participant's hat, so long as the goal is in the public interest. "Frequently, nobody is looking out for the public, whereas you have all sorts of lobbyists working for moneyed groups," he says.

In between these conflicting views are those of Edward Barrett, until recently dean of Columbia University's Graduate School of Journalism. He finds reporters' double role "very disturbing" but "wouldn't put down a blanket prohibition against it." He does feel, though, that the reporter "has an obligation to disclose his involvement to his editors and probably to his readers." Mr. Barrett concedes that "finding a way to do this presents difficulties," but suggests "one possibility might be a notation at the end of the story telling of the reporter's participation."

While this probably would discourage many officeholders from cooperating and almost surely would lessen the impact of many such stories, it certainly would provide readers with intriguing and possibly mountainous footnotes if the full details were included. Consider, for example, the long and arduous adventures of Whitey Watzman:

In April 1967, Mr. Watzman wrote for the Cleveland Plain Dealer a 10-part series based on little-noticed reports by the General Accounting Office, Congress' watchdog agency, which assailed Pentagon waste. The GAO, in spot checks over 10 years, had uncovered $130 million in overcharges by defense companies on certain types of negotiated, noncompetitive contracts that now total about $5 billion a year.

The GAO verdict and the thrust of the Watzman series: The Pentagon wasn't enforcing the Truth-in-Negotiations Act, which requires the negotiating companies to furnish accurate, complete and up-to-date cost estimates. The GAO urged the department to adopt one regulation requiring companies to furnish supporting evidence for cost figures and, touchier still, another regulation letting department auditors peek at company records after jobs were done to see if original estimates and final costs jibed.

An Important Phone Call

But despite heavy play on page one, the Plain Dealer series received no notice outside Cleveland. "That was when we decided to begin a lengthy campaign to get more attention for this," Mr. Watzman says.

Among the first steps was a phone call by Mr. Watzman, whose paper has the largest circulation in Ohio (nearly 400,000 daily and about 540,000 Sundays) to the office of Ohio's Sen. Stephen Young, of Cleveland. "Whitey spoke to me," says Herbert Jolovitz, Sen. Young's administrative assistant.

"He said he thought it would help if a speech were made. I took it up with the Senator, and he liked the idea."

On April 20, Sen. Young delivered a Senate speech criticizing the Pentagon, praising Whitey Watzman, calling for a Congressional investigation and inserting the Watzman series in the Congressional Record. The next morning's Plain Dealer carried a story headlined "Young Asks Defense Dept. Buying Probe."

"Anybody can get stuff in the Congressional Record," Mr. Watzman says. "But at least it was giving some added circulation to the story."

At about that time, he recalls, "I had heard that Sen. Proxmire's subcommittee was going to hold hearings in this general area, so I called up." He spoke to Ray Ward, a staff man on Wisconsin Democrat Proxmire's economy in government subcommittee, and suggested that the truth-in-negotiations issue be included in hearings scheduled for the following month. He got no commitment.

An additional tactic seemed to be needed, and the Plain Dealer's Washington bureau chief, John Leacacos, conferred with the paper's publisher and editor, Thomas Vail. At Mr. Leacacos' suggestion, it was decided that copies would be made of the Watzman series, and on April 26 they were sent, along with a covering letter by Publisher Vail, to all 26 members of Ohio's Congressional delegation, plus some other influential Washingtonians. Mr. Vail's letter said the Plain Dealer

couldn't understand Congress' unawareness of the charges aired in the Watzman stories and asked for any reaction the Ohioans might have.

"We have the same right as any other concerned citizens, and we did what they would do —wrote to our Congressmen," Mr. Watzman says. "What we did beyond that was in furtherance of our objective to cast light on and correct a bad situation. The test in my mind is whether you do this on behalf of a special interest group or on behalf of the public."

Among those receiving the Vail letter was Ray Ward, who showed it and the Watzman series to Sen. Proxmire. The Wisconsin Democrat immediately decided to include the truth-in-negotiations issue in his subcommittee hearings, and he brushed up on the subject in a talk with Mr. Watzman.

Prospects looked brighter. Whitey Watzman arrived at the mid-May hearings anticipating that the wire services and publications with national circulations would at last latch on to his story. But he was in for a letdown. Sen. Proxmire's truth-in-negotiations quizzing came late in each of the hearing sessions, and by that time other reporters of consequence had left the hearing room. So except for Plain Dealer stories on the GAO and Sen. Proxmire attacking Pentagon officials, plus an editorial praising the Senator, there still was hardly a peep about the dispute.

It seemed obvious to Mr. Watzman that other strategies were necessary, and he decided to speak to Republican Reps.

William Minshall of Cleveland and Jackson Betts of Findlay, Ohio. To them he made a new suggestion: A resolution by Ohio's GOP Congressmen.

Seeking More Drama

The resolution was introduced to the group by Rep. Betts, explained by Rep. Minshall, adopted by all 19 Ohio GOP Congressmen and reported in the May 23 Plain Dealer: "19 Ohioans Call McNamara Lax." Citing the Watzman series again, the resolution urged the GOP leadership to press for action to halt Pentagon waste of contract funds.

Though the Plain Dealer noted that this was the first time that the 19 legislators, making up the House's biggest GOP delegation, had "spoken publicly as a group on a major controversy," it was an exclusive story again for the Plain Dealer, the last thing the paper wanted. Clearly, something still more dramatic was needed. It was then that Whitey Watzman conceived of his legislation.

So Whitey wrote letters to Rep. Minshall and Sen. Proxmire, proposing his bill. They liked it. They asked the GAO to draft a measure specifically granting the Pentagon the record-checking authority, and on June 6 identical bills were introduced in the House and Senate.

"It was my bill in the sense that I suggested it, but it was very much the Minshall-Proxmire bill in the more important sense that they were the capable lawmakers who quickly comprehended the need and did

the hard fighting," Mr. Watzman remarks.

New Developments

Eleven days later, the Pentagon took its first step, in response to the quizzing at the May Proxmire hearings: It proposed, and later adopted, regulations requiring negotiating companies to submit supporting data for their cost figures. But the touchier record-peeking question raised by the Minshall-Proxmire bill remained unresolved. On this, there was divided opinion at the Pentagon; auditors there were eager to look into defense company books, but procurement officials were opposed, saying they feared contractors would feel second-guessed if their records were open to scrutiny after a noncompetitive fixed-price contract had been negotiated.

Though the House Armed Services Committee had referred the Minshall-Proxmire bill to the Pentagon for comment, none arrived, and so no hearings were scheduled on the bill. New developments were needed, and they soon came:

—Sen. Young, on advice of Mr. Watzman, asked the GAO for additional reports on Pentagon waste; he got them and delivered another Senate speech.

—On their own, Sen. Proxmire announced the resumption of his subcommittee hearings, the GAO submitted favorable comment on the Minshall-Proxmire bill and Democratic Rep. L. Mendel Rivers, chairman of the House Armed Services Committee, ordered a subcommittee investigation of the Truth-in-Negotiations Act.

—Republican Congressman

Charles Whalen of Dayton, Ohio, got hold of more GAO reports at Mr. Watzman's urging; when he saw them, he decided to make a House speech. Rep. Frank Bow of Canton, Ohio, after a talk with Whitey Watzman, criticized the Pentagon in his newsletter to constituents. Whitey phoned Rep. Minshall ("I knew what he would say, of course") and ran a story headlined "Minshall Charges Stalling on Truth Bill." He called the Pentagon for reaction to this charge and received no comment; he wrote that, too.

—Dayton's Rep. Whalen, a member of the Armed Services Committee, introduced another bill identical to the Minshall-Proxmire measure. And Democratic Rep. Porter Hardy Jr. of Virginia, presiding over the panel's investigating subcommittee, attacked the Defense Department for still not submitting comment on the measures.

Finally, on Nov. 2, Assistant Defense Secretary Thomas Morris delivered to Rep. Minshall and Sen. Proxmire copies of a new Pentagon regulation requiring a clause in all affected contracts allowing department auditors to open company books; at the same time, the Pentagon dropped any opposition to the Minshall-Proxmire bill. Whitey Watzman's strategy had worked.

"I didn't care that much about the bill any more," says Mr. Watzman. But Rep. Minshall and Sen. Proxmire still cared, maintaining that a Pentagon regulation could be withdrawn at any time. With the legislators still pushing for it to become law, the measure cleared the House Armed Services panel last April 26 and was adopted in the full House on May 6.

3   Internal Control

Horace Greeley launched the New York **Tribune** in 1841.   Greeley was greatly taken with the philosophy of French socialist Charles Fourier. For five years he preached Fourierism wherever he went—and so did the **Tribune.**   Then he lost interest in the movement, and his paper never mentioned it again.   Greeley was a teetotaler; the **Tribune** fought for prohibition.   Greeley was opposed to capital punishment; the **Tribune** campaigned for its abolition.   Greeley was a bitter enemy of slavery; so was the **Tribune.**

Greeley was a typical nineteenth-century publisher: He viewed his newspaper as an extension of himself.   Today's metropolitan publishers and broadcasters are a different breed.   They are far more likely to be found in the front office than in the newsroom.   They look after the financial health of their companies and let their professional employees look after the news.

Yet even today the mass-media owner retains almost absolute power to control news coverage—and from time to time he uses it.   Often the economic interests of the owner dictate a "business policy"—treat that advertiser well in your story.   Sometimes the individual quirks of the owner dictate a "personal policy"—write more about that movie star. And occasionally the ideological convictions of the owner dictate a "political policy"—ignore the speeches of that candidate. Reporters who want to keep their jobs carefully adhere to these unwritten policies, even if the owner never shows his face in the newsroom.

Most media owners today are, first and foremost, businessmen. Their policies are remarkably similar; they may well cater to the same advertisers, disapprove of some politicians, and even enjoy the same movie stars. To the extent that media owners control media content, therefore, they are likely to produce a consistent bias. Horace Greeley was a meddler but also an individualist. The average publisher today meddles somewhat less, but far more predictably.

Though owners are potentially the most important individuals in the mass media, most use their power sparingly. The vast majority of the important day-to-day news decisions are made by the staff—by reporters and editors. Certain positions within media bureaucracies inevitably involve tremendous influence over news content. Many of these are relatively low-level positions, in terms of status and salary.

Consider, for example, the following critically important media "gatekeepers," who determine what news "gets through" to the public:

- The telegraph editor, who seects less than a tenth of the available wire-service stories and puts them into his newspaper.
- The headline writer, who controls the reader's first thoughts on a topic and determines whether or not he will read further.
- The assignment editor, who decides what his reporters will cover and what they will ignore.
- The film editor, who takes twenty minutes of a radio or TV story and cuts it down to a minute or less—of his own choosing.
- The reporter, who decides which sources to talk to, which facts to include, and which order to put them in.

Though media owners are consistently conservative, media gatekeepers may be almost as consistently liberal. This fact has received less attention from the critics, but it is just as dangerous as the other. Even more dangerous is the fact that they are largely unaware of their power.

The selection that follows recounts the preparation of a single day's television newscast. As you read the description, ask yourself three questions: Who has the power in this local newsroom? Are they aware of it? Are they using it wisely?

FRANK ALLEN PHILPOT

The Making of a Newscast

KXXX-TV is a major San Francisco television station, owned and operated by one of the three networks. It has a news staff of approximately
30. KXXX has done fairly well with its news—although this depends to
some extent on which rating service you give the most credence to.
A. C. Nielsen puts KXXX news in a strong second place behind KYYY.
The American Research Bureau has KXXX and KZZZ almost tied for
second.

There are three primary inputs into the news operation and about
half a dozen secondary inputs.

Primary Inputs

Wires: The station subscribes to six wires: both the AP and UPI
national wires, both radio wires, the UPI sports wire and the UPI state
wire. This combination obviously produces immense duplication. When
I asked the assignment editor why the station took this combination of
wires, he looked at me blankly and said, "That's all there are." I put the
same question to the news director and his response was, "That's all we
need." Apparently no one has given any consideration to the possibility
of dropping one of the radio wires, for example, and substituting one of
the supplementary services.

Used by permission. At the request of the news manager, the identity of this
station and the names of its employees have been disguised.

Networks: The national network news department collects more tape and film reports each day than it can use on its half-hour news program, so the out-takes—or extra stories—are offered as a syndicated service to all the network affiliates for local use.

The producer of the KXXX evening news leaves a certain number of holes for network material when he first puts together the rough schedule early in the afternoon. At 3:30 he receives a summary of the material, but the actual feed does not come over the network lines until 4:30. On the basis of the summary, he chooses two or three items to include in his program and gives directions to the tape editors to take these out of the feed when it comes. He does not look at this material until the program goes on the air at 6:00.

Staff reporters: KXXX-TV has seven street reporters plus two full-time trainee reporters. These reporters almost always work as a team with one of the station's six film cameramen. The nine reporters are divided over seven days and two shifts so that at any one time there are no more than five reporters available. All are on general assignment.

Secondary Inputs

Newspapers: Three newspapers are examined by the assignment editor each day—the *San Francisco Chronicle,* the *San Francisco Examiner,* and the *Oakland Tribune.* These are the major papers in the area; they are used primarily as sources of leads and normally stories are not re-written directly out of the papers.

UPI Unifax: The station subscribes to the UPI picture service and receives approximately 100 pictures per day—but these are very seldom used on the air. The importance of "live" action is so ingrained in the thinking of the staff that they normally just don't think in terms of still pictures.

Los Angeles news: KXXX receives the second half hour of the local news program of the network's Los Angeles affiliate. The network lines are free for only an hour and the feed of the network news takes the other half of the hour. In special situations KXXX can ask the L.A. station for a particular piece of film.

Other stations: News film is occasionally exchanged with affiliates in Sacramento and Fresno.

Network news: The half-hour network news is fed by the network at 5:00 P.M. but delayed by KXXX until 7:00 P.M. Often actualities from this show are used on the 11:00 P.M. news, and occasionally also on the 6:00 P.M. program.

Other network feeds: During special events such as a space shot, a national funeral, etc., KXXX tapes the network feed and edits excerpts to use on its news programs.

According to the assignment editor and the news director, Monday, November 24, 1969, the day I visited the station, was a fairly typical day for their news operation.

7:00 A.M. I arrive at the station. The only person in the newsroom is Dave Mitchell, a reporter who comes in at 6:30 and does two five-minute radio-type newscasts during the morning. These are pulled right off the wire and involve virtually no preparation.

7:05 Gene Gilbert, the assignment editor, comes in. His first action after taking off his coat is to turn on the TV monitor in the newsroom to the morning KXXX program. This is a two-hour call-in talk program and guests are often a source of news interviews.

7:15 Gilbert looks over the wire services' lists of events scheduled for San Francisco today and makes notes on which press conferences he wants to send reporters to. Next he looks through his future file for story possibilities. Gilbert commutes from the suburbs every day and reads the *Chronicle* on his way into the city.

7:22 A cameraman checks in by two-way radio on his way to work and asks if anything is happening yet. Gilbert tells him no.

7:55 A reporter calls in sick. Since one reporter is on vacation this makes Gilbert short two men. Only three regular reporters will be available for street work most of the day.

Senator Thomas Eagleton (Dem., Mo.) is a guest on the station's morning talk show and has been discussing Spiro Agnew's recent attacks on TV news. Gilbert calls one of the cameramen over and tells him that he wants an interview with Eagleton after the program finishes. The cameraman goes downstairs to set up his equipment in the station lobby.

8:05 Gilbert and reporter Mitchell discuss the shortage of reporters. A group of Indians have been camped on Alcatraz for about a week and Gilbert is undecided as to whether he should send a reporter out to the island today. Mitchell suggests that he could do a one-minute voice report based on wire-service information over silent film left over from last week's coverage of the Indian story. This would conserve manpower but give the impression that the station had a reporter on the story today. Gilbert likes the idea but holds off on a final decision.

8:20 Gilbert begins to get nervous because he doesn't have a reporter yet to interview Eagleton. (Mitchell is tied up preparing another five-minute newscast for 8:25.)

8:25 Another reporter, Chuck Black, comes in and Gilbert asks him to go down and interview Eagleton. Black has about five minutes to look over the *Chronicle* and consider some questions for the Senator.

8:25 Mitchell does his five-minute newscast.

8:30 Gilbert cleans off a large plastic assignment board and writes in the first assignment for the day—the interview with Eagleton.

The talk show concludes and "Anniversary Game" begins on the mon itor. After about 20 minutes the banality gets through to one of the trainee reporters and the set is turned off.

8:45 A second assignment goes up on the board: an interview with State Senator Milton Marks, who was also a guest on the talk show. Gilbert remarks to Black, "It would be rude to ignore Marks if we're going to interview Eagleton." The assignment editor is obviously pleased to have two pieces of film this early on a day he is short on reporters.

Two cameramen wander in and discuss with Gilbert the way the weekend crew handled several stories. The consensus is that the Sunday night news was not very good. One cameraman suggests a possible story on educational reform at St. Mary's college. (The *Chronicle* had a feature on the subject today.) After a few minutes it becomes clear that the cameraman's primary interest is in "shooting some of those great campus scenes" and that he doesn't have much feel for the news value of the story.

9:00 By now there are about a half dozen people in the newsroom including one of the trainee reporters, two regular reporters, Gilbert, a secretary, and a cameraman.

Gilbert asks the secretary to call the Japanese embassy and ask for Premier Sato's schedule for the day. He thinks he had one last week but apparently has lost it.

9:15 Gilbert assigns a cameraman to go to the St. Francis Hotel to shoot some film of the opening of a conference on "Man and His Environment," sponsored by the United States Commission for UNESCO. A reporter (Dave Mitchell) will meet him there later in the morning. I go with the cameraman to see how things are done outside the office.

On our way to the St. Francis I ask the cameraman what he will look for and how he will decide what to shoot when we get to the conference. "Well, we just want to show that a conference took place," he replies. "I'll shoot some overall shots of the people and when Dave comes maybe he'll want to interview someone."

10:00 We arrive at the conference and the cameraman shoots about 1¼ minutes of film of the audience and of Arthur Godfrey at the podium. The conference planners have arranged a press conference so after the opening remarks we move on to the pressroom, ignoring the panel discussions where papers will be presented.

The first person presented at the press conference is Miss Louise Gore, a Maryland state senator and a U.S. ambassador to UNESCO. Some of the broadcast reporters in the back of the room make a few snide remarks about the quality of her presentation but they keep asking questions and the cameras keep rolling. Dave Perlman, science reporter or the *Chronicle,* walks in, notes what is going on and promptly goes back to the serious program.

After 30 endless minutes Miss Gore steps down and Arthur Godfrey comes on. Mr. Godfrey says some nice things about the need for conservation and for awareness of pollution problems, but his remarks really have nothing to do with the substance of the conference. He could come into town any day, call a press conference, say the same things and receive just as much coverage. Meanwhile, scientists, government officials and educators are in other parts of the hotel talking about serious environmental problems—and they are talking in layman's language, not scientific jargon. (I picked up copies of some of the conference papers as we went out.)

When KXXX carried the story at 6:00 P.M. it consisted of about 45 seconds of film from the opening session (sponsorship was incorrectly attributed directly to UNESCO) and about two minutes of Arthur Godfrey's comments (edited so that the point of his remarks was partially obscured).

11:15 The press conference is over and we head back to the office. The film is dropped off at a lab across from the station and will be processed and returned for editing in about half an hour.

Dave Mitchell prepares a "poop" sheet listing the film shot and the general nature of the event and leaves this for a writer-producer who will prepare the story. Normally two reporters appear live on the evening news program. They write the copy for the stories they cover. But when another reporter covers a story, the copy is written by a writer-producer. The reporter's role is thus primarily to appear on film as the representative of the station and ask questions.

Three items have been added to the assignment board while I was gone: "Submarine," "Schools" and "Gavin." The first is the result of a visit by a member of the Lockheed public relations staff. He came to the station with a model of a new rescue submarine and a piece of animated film describing its operation. The second item is an attempt to put a local angle on a national event. The Apollo-12 crew is due to splash down today and one of the trainee reporters has been sent to an elementary school to get reactions from young children. The third item is another staged "pseudo-event"—General James Gavin is in town and is going to hold a press conference. (For some reason, it never came off.)

11:45 Bill Stevens, one of the writer-producers, looks at the film of Black's interviews with Eagleton and Marks. He times each segment with a stopwatch and tells the film editor where to cut the film.

1:00 P.M. The assistant news director (Herb Marks) and the producer of the 6:00 P.M. program (Jim Stewart) confer and agree on a tentative run-down for the evening news. This is roughly equivalent to a news-paper layout. They begin with the list of commercials and the estab-lished segments (local and national weather, the general manager's editorial, etc.), then arrange the stories they have and think they will have into some sort of pattern. The final arrangement is determined by several factors: how important the story is, whether it has film or tape, and who did the story. (If a reporter has two or three stories on the show the producer tries not to place all his pieces back to back.)

After the producer and the assistant news director agree on the run-down it is put up on a large plastic board next to the assignment board. Ray Thomas, anchorman for the evening news, comes in. Thomas is the most visible part of the station's news program but his only contri-bution is to write the headlines and one or two minutes of national news that open the show.

1:30 The first edition of the *Examiner* is brought in by the secretary. The front page contains a story about a new police garage which has been under construction for an unusually long time and which seems to have a number of defects—i.e., the ceilings are too low to accommodate police vans, fire doors are blocked by window boxes, etc. Gilbert sends out a reporter and photographer to do a story. They call back in about half an hour and report that they don't really think there is a story. "The garage is locked," the reporter says, "and there's not anything to take a picture of." The assignment editor accepts this assessment and tells the crew to follow Japanese Premier Sato for the afternoon and get a story on his tour of the city.

2:00 Gilbert tells Dave Mitchell to go ahead with a voice report on the Indian situation on Alcatraz, based on a telephone call to the care-taker's wife. This will run over file footage to give the impression a reporter was on the scene.

2:15 The first edition of the Oakland *Tribune* comes in and Gilbert skims it for leads. Nothing interesting turns up.

2:30 The San Francisco Board of Supervisors has called a press con-ference to announce the appointment of one of its members to the Board of Directors of Bay Area Rapid Transit. (This supervisor had just lost his seat in an election.) A reporter-photographer team is dispatched.

3:30 Jim Stewart, the producer of the six o'clock news, updates the rundown board by adding items from the network budget. The psy-chological center of the newsroom has begun to shift from Gilbert's desk to Stewart's.

3:45 A cameraman discusses with Gilbert the possibility of shooting some film later in the week of industrial plants in the area that put out an unusual amount of smoke. This is one of the few examples of station-initiated stories I saw during my visit. Notice the emphasis on the simple visual angle—smoke pouring out of factories. Meanwhile the station is, for all practical purposes, ignoring the UNESCO Commission's conference on environmental pollution problems.

4:00 Writers begin to put together a script. The pace of activity is picking up perceptibly.

4:20 Gilbert cleans off his desk, makes notes for his future file and leaves for home.

5:05 A quality of edgy excitement begins to appear in the newsroom. One piece of film is late, and one reporter who hasn't finished his story is downstairs having his picture taken by the promotion department.

5:20 Jim Stewart—now the clear boss in the newsroom—begins to take pieces of copy from different writers and reporters and starts making up a master script.

5:35 The video-tape department has been recording the live Apollo-12 coverage the station has been carrying from the network, and Stewart had planned to use some of this tape as his lead story. Now the tape editors report that they will not be able to edit the film in time for the 6:00 P.M. deadline. Unhappily, Stewart decides to take the Apollo-12 story off the tape of the network news show. This means the viewers who watch the 90-minute news block all the way through will see exactly the same story in the local and national news.

5:40 Reporters who will appear on the air put on their KXXX-monogrammed sports jackets, and those with 5 o'clock shadows shave quickly. Bob Fisher, the sports director, brings in the sports material.

5:54 The staff moves downstairs to the studio and control room.

6:00 The show is on the air.

Anchorman Thomas introduces the Apollo-12 story and gives the verbal cue for the tape. Nothing happens. The tape room wasn't ready. He ad-libs for 45 seconds and then the tape is rolled.

Commercial.

Chuck Black does a story on the appointment of Supervisor Blake to the BART Board of Directors. Includes about one minute of film.

Alcatraz. Dave Mitchell does the voice report over file footage.

Van Anderson reports on Premier Sato's tour of the city. The gist of the story is that the premier whizzed by all the city's important landmarks in two hours and the reporters had trouble keeping up with his motorcade. This story took about two minutes (relatively long for TV news) and was in the fourth position. The next morning the *Chronicle* gave it three paragraphs on page 9.

Commercials. (Four of them.)

Thomas does a story on the Song My massacre. Rewrite of wire copy.

Interview with the wife of a serviceman being held prisoner by the North Vietnamese. Network item.

Thomas does 30 seconds on the state of Paris non-negotiations and on a current battle in Vietnam.

Film of Attorney General Mitchell saying that poverty is no excuse for crime. Another network item.

Interview with Eagleton.

More commercials.

Jerry Jennings does the story on the conference on environmental problems sponsored by the U.S. Commission for UNESCO. The defects in this story were noted earlier.

Thomas reports that a murder suspect has been picked up in Palm Springs. Off wire.

National weather report.

Commercials.

Regional weather report.

Rescue submarine story. The Lockheed P.R. department will be happy tonight.

Tape of a movie review Rolfe Peters did before he went on vacation.

Bob Fisher reports on the Oakland Raiders game over the weekend.

Commercial.

More sports.

Twenty-second story on a San Jose bus strike. Rewrite off wire.

Interview with State Senator Milton Marks.

Statement by an official of the California Teachers Association about tax reform. Another press conference.

Commercial.

Jerry Jennings does the first of a three-part series on housing problems in the Bay area. The story runs just over four minutes and consists of interviews with three "experts" on the local housing situation. (The experts are not audibly identified but one was apparently a real-estate salesman.) Their common conclusion was that inflation was the cause of the entire problem. Although I have some personal doubts as to whether the problem is quite that simple, this was the best piece of journalism on the program.

Statement by economist Walter Heller. Another press conference.

Commercials.

Local weather report.

One-minute recap of major stories.

6:56 Close of newscast and introduction of the station editorial, which is prepared by the general manager's office.

7:00 The staff moves back upstairs and breaks up for dinner. Van Anderson and Bob Fisher will be back later in the evening to do the

1:00 P.M. news. Essentially the late newscast is an edited combination
f the 6:00 P.M. local program and the 7:00 P.M. network news. New
ilm or tape is seldom available and since there is only one-third as much
ime, new material would be difficult to work in.

Looking back over the day it seems to me that television news is more
usceptible to the lure of what Daniel Boorstin has called "pseudo-
vents" than are newspapers. By my count, the KXXX reporters pre-
ared 10 local stories on the day I watched the operation. The rest of
he program consisted of sports, weather, commercials and material sup-
lied by the network and wire services. If we consider the appearance
f Senators Eagleton and Marks on the talk show as a form of press
onference, then 7 of the 10 stories came out of press conferences. Of
he three non–press conference stories, one was the non-report from
Alcatraz and another was a worthless piece of film about how hard it is
o keep up with a Japanese prime minister's motorcade. That left one
tory—the housing piece—that constituted solid journalism. A depress-
ngly low score, in my opinion, for a one-hour news program produced
y a network o-and-o station in a major market. (Which is not to suggest that this performance is not typical. Unfortunately I am afraid it is
ery typical.) . . .

4 Monopoly Control

The concept of freedom of the press is based on the conviction that truth somehow emerges from the conflict of many voices. But freedom can become a dangerous luxury when the number of voices falls too low. Today, control of the media is largely concentrated in the hands of a few huge monopolies, run by media "barons" of incredible power.

There are four important varieties of media monopolies: chains and networks, cross-media ownerships, joint operating agreements, and conglomerates. Consider the following statistics.

- Just under half the newspapers in the United States are owned by chains—that is, by companies that also own other newspapers.
- Nearly three-quarters of all the television stations in the country are chain-owned, and roughly 90 percent of the commercial stations are affiliated with one of the three networks.
- A single owner controls at least one TV station and one newspaper in thirty-four of the nation's fifty largest cities, giving tremendous power to these cross-media owners.
- Every VHF television station in eleven states is owned by either a newspaper or a chain.
- At least forty-six newspapers in twenty-three cities pool their pro-

fits or otherwise participate in noncompetitive joint-operating agreements.

• Many newspapers and broadcast stations, and most major magazines and book publishers, are owned by conglomerates with interests outside the communications industry.

Every form of media monopoly, at least in theory, cuts down the diversity of viewpoints available to the public. Every form of media monopoly makes it that much easier for the monopolist to slant the news and gives him the economic clout to squelch the opposition—if he has any opposition left. To be sure, there are some monopoly newspapers and broadcast stations that do a better job than most of the competitive ones. But we are at the monopolist's mercy. Next year he may be less trustworthy.

The trend toward media combination might be less worrisome if there were an ever-increasing number of media outlets. Unfortunately, this is not the case. For economic as well as technological reasons, the number of broadcast stations throughout much of the country has pretty much reached its maximum (barring cable developments). And the number of metropolitan newspapers is actually declining; there are fewer daily papers in the country today than there were in 1890.

Take New York City. The city has six commercial VHF television stations—all the FCC will allow. Three of them are owned by the three networks. Two others are owned by chains (Metromedia and RKO General). And the sixth station is owned by the New York **Daily News**. The largest city in the United States does not have a single independently owned VHF television station. There are several independent UHF stations in New York, but the audience for UHF (channels 14 through 80) is still very small.

As for newspapers, New York boasted fifteen of them in 1890. By 1965 the number was down to six: the **Times, Herald Tribune**, and **Daily News** in the morning; the **Post, World-Telegram & Sun**, and **Journal-American** in the afternoon. The hyphenated names give some indication of the diversity that had been. Then, in 1966, the **Herald Tribune** merged with the **World-Telegram & Sun** and the **Journal-American** to form a single afternoon paper. It was named the **World-Journal-Tribune**, and within a year it too had folded. New York now survives with only three daily newspapers—the **Times**, the **Daily News**, and the **Post**.

The selection that follows traces the history of the ill-fated **World-Journal-Tribune**. It is a history of merger after merger, monopoly upon monopoly. When the W.J.T. died in 1967, thirty-eight other newspapers died with it. Hearst's **Journal** died. Day's **Sun** died. Bennett's **Herald**

died. Greeley's **Tribune** died. Webster's **American Minerva** died. Pul
itzer's **World** died. And many would agree that freedom of the pres
died a little too.

DANIEL J. LEAB

A Genealogy of the New York Merger

1. The Journal-American Family

THE DAILY STAR: Published as "the successor to the Old Sun" from
January 25, 1868, by ex-employees of *The Sun*, who believed that the
latter's sale to C. A. Dana meant its transformation into a "Radical Jour
nal." Consolidated with THE DEMOCRAT, May 14, 1871. Bought by Frank
A. Munsey (1854–1925) in January, 1891, and changed (February 1) to
THE DAILY CONTINENT, a pioneer tabloid. After four months, became the
full-size MORNING ADVERTISER under John A. Cockerill (1845–1896), a
former Pulitzer editor. Sold to Hearst April 1, 1897, for $125,000.

THE DEMOCRAT: Started August 15, 1868, by Marcus M. (Brick) Pomeroy
(1833–1896), to support "a white man's government for white men" and
other Democratic programs. Sold to THE STAR May 12, 1871.

MORNING JOURNAL: Established November 16, 1882, by Albert Pulitzer
(1851–1909), Joseph's brother, on $25,000 capital. Sold to John R. Mc-
Lean (1848–1916), publisher of the *Cincinnati Enquirer,* early in 1895 for
$1,000,000. McLean sold to William Randolph Hearst (1863–1951) on
September 25, 1895, for $180,000; began publication under Hearst
November 7, 1895. Spawned the NEW YORK EVENING JOURNAL, September
28, 1896. Published as the JOURNAL AND ADVERTISER after Hearst's purchase of MORNING ADVERTISER for an Associated Press franchise. Became
the NEW YORK JOURNAL AND AMERICAN after public reaction against
Hearst's violent attacks on President McKinley before assassination. Be-

Reprinted from *The Columbia Journalism Review,* Spring, 1966, 4–7. Used by
permission of the author and the publisher.

ame the NEW YORK AMERICAN (1903–1937). On June 24, 1937, bankers o whom Hearst had yielded financial management killed the AMERICAN. Part of features and AP franchise went to Hearst's MIRROR (1924–1964) and the rest to the EVENING JOURNAL. Merged paper, eventually called NEW YORK JOURNAL-AMERICAN, ceased publication April 24, 1966, and OURNAL became part of name of new afternoon paper.

2. The Herald Tribune Family

THE SUN: Established September 3, 1833, by Benjamin H. Day (1810–1889); became city's first successful penny paper. Sold to Day's brother-in-law, Moses Y. Beach (1800–1868), in 1838. Sold to C. A. Dana (1819–1897) and associates January 25, 1868. Company also issued EVENING SUN from March 17, 1887. Both papers bought by Munsey June 30, 1916, for $2,468,000. The morning SUN was consolidated with another Munsey paper to form THE SUN AND NEW YORK PRESS on July 3, 1916. Within the month it became simply THE SUN. Combined with THE NEW YORK HERALD on February 1, 1920, and appeared with combined name until September 30, 1920, when THE SUN disappeared. (For chronology of *Evening Sun*, see below.)

MORNING HERALD: Started May 6, 1835, by James Gordon Bennett (1795–1872). Management passed to J. G. Bennett, Jr. (1841–1918) in 1866. Declined after 1900, and sold by Bennett estate January 17, 1920, to Munsey, who paid $4,000,000 for HERALD, *Telegram*, and Paris *Herald*. Combined February 1, 1920, with the morning SUN. Called THE SUN AND THE NEW YORK HERALD until September 30, 1920, then became again THE NEW YORK HERALD. Sold to Reid family's TRIBUNE, with Paris edition, for $5,000,000 March 17, 1924.

NEW YORK TRIBUNE: Founded April 10, 1841, by Horace Greeley (1811–1872). After Greeley's death, control fell to the managing editor, Whitelaw Reid (1837–1912), and the paper remained with the Reid family eighty-five years. In 1924 Munsey attempted to buy it; instead, the Reids bought his *Herald*. The NEW YORK HERALD TRIBUNE appeared on March 18, 1924. In August, 1958, the Reids transferred control of the paper to John Hay Whitney, American ambassador in London. Merged into new joint corporation with *Journal-American* and *World-Telegram*, April, 1966.

THE PRESS: First published December 1, 1887, by Frank Hatton (1846–1895) a former postmaster general, and Robert P. Porter (1852–1917), a

Heading for the last merger

Starting at right, the *Review* presents the family background of the merger of New York City newspapers, which was intended to create on April 25 a new afternoon newspaper called the *World Journal* and on May 1 a new Sunday newspaper called the *World Journal Tribune* (not to mention a new morning newspaper under the old name of *Herald Tribune*). Because newspaper unions, unhappy over the fate of their members, blocked the way, these events did not occur on schedule.

Behind each of these new entities is a genealogy of foundings, founderings, and mergers, each combination entered as reluctantly as that of 1966. In part, the chart is offered for the record.

More important, one can see reflected in the chart the travails of an industry perpetually insecure and murderously competitive, abused periodically by unscrupulous manipulators. Especially heavy is the hand of Frank A. Munsey, who handled newspapers, in William Allen White's famous words, with "the talent of a meat packer, the morals of a money changer and the manners of an undertaker." He thrust himself into the New York newspaper field from 1891 until his death in 1925. He was the embalmer of three papers in the *Herald Tribune* lineage, and of two more in the *World-Telegram & Sun* branch. Certainly, he stabilized the field to an extent, but he also showed that merely cutting down the number of papers is not in itself the road to permanent prosperity or good journalism.

One can also see in the chart the cycles of foundings and mergers: the wave of beginnings up to 1841, the first popular press; the second wave after the Civil War; a third wave riding on the technological advances of the 1880's. There was also the tabloid wave of the 1920's, but for the older papers shown here that decade was the era of Munsey.

Finally, one can see here forgotten nameplates, representing the efforts of hundreds of forgotten editors, publishers, and reporters. Their newspapers lasted anywhere from four months to nearly 130 years. But in the end, none sustained corporate life and now the chart has narrowed to one entry.

A GENEALOGY OF THE NEW YORK MERGER

This chart shows in detail the antecedents of the newspapers involved in the three-way merger in New York this spring, starting with the founding of the American Minerva in 1793. It can best be understood as showing the lineage of three families: the Journal-American at top, the Herald Tribune in the middle, the World-Telegram at the bottom. The nameplates, many of them nearly forgotten, are reproduced from originals. The dates next to them show the year of founding or merger. Details of the history of each newspaper are shown in the directory on pages 6 and 7.

Compiled, collected, and designed by Daniel J. Leab

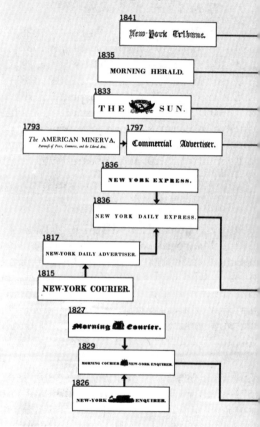

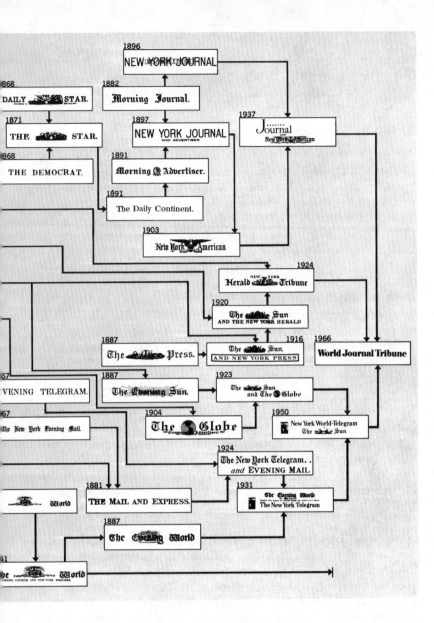

1896
NEW YORK JOURNAL

868
DAILY STAR.

1882
Morning Journal.

1937
Journal and New York American

1871
THE STAR.

1897
NEW YORK JOURNAL
AND ADVERTISER.

868
THE DEMOCRAT.

1891
Morning Advertiser.

1891
The Daily Continent.

1903
New York American

1924
Herald NEW YORK Tribune

1920
The Sun.
AND THE NEW YORK HERALD

1887
The Press.

1916
The Sun.
AND NEW YORK PRESS

1966
World Journal Tribune

57
EVENING TELEGRAM.

1887
The Evening Sun.

1923
The Sun
and The Globe

67
The New York Evening Mail.

1904
The Globe
COMMERCIAL Advertiser.

1950
New York World-Telegram
The Sun

1924
The New York Telegram..
and EVENING MAIL

1881
THE MAIL AND EXPRESS.

1931
The Evening World
The New York Telegram

World

1887
The Evening World

61
he World
MORNING COURIER AND NEW-YORK ENQUIRER.

journalist. Munsey bought the paper on September 16, 1912, for $1,000-
000. On July 3, 1916, Munsey combined it with the morning SUN, the
name disappeared on July 30.

3. The World-Telegram Family

AMERICAN MINERVA: First issued December 9, 1793, guided by Noah
Webster, supported Alexander Hamilton. Quarrels among proprietors
led to suspension on September 30, 1797, and founding by Webster of a
successor, the evening COMMERCIAL ADVERTISER, on October 2, 1797.
Lasted until January 30, 1904, under that name. Became THE GLOBE AND
COMMERCIAL ADVERTISER on Feburary 1, 1904, after promotion campaign.
Bought for $2,000,000 on May 29, 1923, by Munsey, and merged six days
later with the evening SUN. Name of GLOBE disappeared March 9, 1924.

COURIER: Established January 10, 1815, by Barent Gardenier, who was
involved in paper's operation until February 19, 1817, when it was taken
over by Theodore Dwight (1764–1846) for the National Republicans. On
April 9, 1817, it appeared as the NEW-YORK DAILY ADVERTISER. After
Dwight's retirement, was merged with politically sympathetic NEW YORK
EXPRESS, November 1, 1836.

NEW YORK EXPRESS: Founded as a morning paper June 20, 1836, by
James Brooks (1810–1873) with $7,500 capital. Absorbed the DAILY AD-
VERTISER later in year. Became in 1864 an evening paper. Brooks joined
by his brother Erastus (1815–1886), who remained with the paper until
1877, when it became, under "Honest" John Kelly (1821–1886), an organ
of Tammany Hall. Consolidated with THE EVENING MAIL December 5,
1881.

NEW YORK EVENING MAIL: Started September 21, 1867, by Charles H.
Sweetser (1841–1871), a newspaperman, and, after various owners, was
sold November, 1877, at a sheriff's sale. Cyrus W. Field (1819–1892),
promoter of the Atlantic cable, took control in 1878 and three years later
bought the EXPRESS for its AP franchise. THE MAIL AND EXPRESS appeared
on November 5, 1881. After its reputation was tarnished in World War I
by collaboration with German propagandists, it was bought for $2,200,000
by Munsey, who combined it with the TELEGRAM on January 28, 1924.
The EVENING MAIL part of the name was dropped on May 17, 1925.

THE EVENING TELEGRAM: James Gordon Bennett, Jr., son of the *Herald's*
founder, started the TELEGRAM independently on July 1, 1867, printing it
on pink paper. Bought with other Bennett papers by Munsey, January

7, 1920; combined with the MAIL four years later. As THE NEW YORK
ELEGRAM, sold to Scripps-Howard, becoming that company's first New
ork venture, February 12, 1927. With Scripps-Howard purchase of the
ORLD, February 26, 1931, became part of NEW YORK WORLD-TELEGRAM.
lame disappeared in merger of 1966.

VENING SUN: First issued March 17, 1887, as offshoot of the morning
un. Sold, with morning Sun, to Munsey in 1916. On June 4, 1923,
lunsey combined Sun with his newly acquired Globe; combined name
sted until March 9, 1924, when title became The Sun. Munsey died in
925; in 1926, William Dewart (1875–1944) took control. On January 5,
950, bought by Scripps-Howard and name added to that of the WORLD-
ELEGRAM. Subordinate for sixteen years, name vanished in the 1966
lerger.

lORNING COURIER: Started by John B. Skillman (c. 1796–1834), hardware
lerchant, May 3, 1827. Sold to his brother-in-law, James Watson Webb
1802–1884), December, 1827. Webb acquired NEW YORK ENQUIRER and
lublished combined paper, May 25, 1829. After printing confession of
lability to change with times, consolidated with THE WORLD, 1861. The
lOURIER and ENQUIRER names were dropped December 29, 1863.

lEW YORK ENQUIRER: Started by Mordecai M. Noah (1785–1851), a Jack-
lonian, July 6, 1826. Costly competition with COURIER led to consolida-
ion in 1827, and Noah soon sold out to Webb. Name survived, with
lOURIER, until dropped by THE WORLD, 1863.

lHE WORLD: Started June 14, 1860, by Alexander Cummings (1810–1879),
ames Spalding (1821–1872), Richard Grant White (1821–1885), as reli-
lious penny paper. After losses, merged with COURIER and ENQUIRER
uly 1, 1861; appeared for two and a half years as THE WORLD AND MORN-
NG COURIER AND NEW YORK ENQUIRER. After succession of owners, THE
lORLD was bought in May, 1883, by Joseph Pulitzer (1847–1911) for
l346,000. Pulitzer began the EVENING WORLD, October 10, 1887. His sons
eceived court permission to break their father's will February 26, 1931,
lnd sold the papers to Roy Howard (1883–1964) of Scripps-Howard for
l5,000,000. Combined EVENING WORLD and TELEGRAM appeared February
l7, 1931; morning WORLD ceased publication. In 1966, name of WORLD
las preserved in new evening newspaper.

5   Advertiser Control

Imagine that you were the vice-president for advertising of Procter & Gamble, a detergent manufacturer that in 1970 spent over $120,000,000 on television advertising alone—most of it for daytime serials. Imagine also that one of your serials was planning an episode in which the heroine goes swimming in detergent-polluted water and suffers a psychotic breakdown because of the filth. You would almost certainly feel tempted to ask the producer to skip that part. And you might well feel cheated if he refused.

As far as we know, P&G does not monitor TV shows before broadcast. But then, as far as we know, no soap opera has ever featured the dangers of detergent pollution. With $120,000,000 of Procter & Gamble's money at stake, no soap opera is likely to do so.

With the exception of books and movies, all the mass media are supported in whole or in part by advertising. The advertiser pays the piper. If the wants to, he can more or less call the tune.

What is surprising is not that advertisers possess this power, but that they use it so sparingly. Advertising boycotts of a newspaper or broadcast station are rare and seldom last longer than a week or two. Ideological or political boycotts are rarer still. The underground press would quickly die if it were not supported by ads from the business establishment it regularly attacks—especially from record companies and the like.

Advertiser control of the media is typically more subtle than this. It finds expression in practices like the following:

- Newspapers often run free publicity "news" for a major advertiser, sometimes on an explicit schedule of so many inches of news for each full-page ad.
- Television performers and even newsmen are often asked to do their own commercials, lending greater credibility and interest to the ads.
- News stories that might embarrass an advertiser are often downplayed or killed.
- Contradictions between paid and unpaid content are avoided; planes do not crash on programs sponsored by TWA.
- Controversial programming that might interfere with uncritical acceptance of the advertising message is avoided.

Over the years, media men have come to know what advertisers expect, and they supply it without questioning. Nobody has to tell a newspaper copy editor to cut the name of the car out of that traffic-accident article. He understands without being told that including the name might embarrass the manufacturer. He understands that embarrassing the manufacturer would be in "bad taste" for the newspaper. He understands that that just is not the sort of thing one business (publishing) does to another business (automotive). He does not have to be threatened or bribed; such tactics would only offend and bewilder him.

Such understandings have the greatest effect on television. A newspaper or magazine advertiser cannot pick the article that will appear next to his ad. A TV advertiser can—and does. A show without advertiser appeal is unlikely to be produced, unlikelier to be broadcast, and unlikeliest to be renewed for a second season.

Not too long ago, NBC President Robert Kintner was asked, "Who is responsible for what appears on network cameras?" "The ultimate responsibility is ours," Kintner replied, "but the ultimate power has to be the sponsor's, because without him you couldn't afford to run a network."

The selection that follows deals with ABC, financially the weakest of the three TV networks. In particular, it deals with ABC's documentaries. Now documentaries—especially controversial ones—have very little appeal for advertisers. The networks run them (reluctantly) to help build prestige, and to keep the Federal Communications Commission happy. In 1969, the selection reports, ABC felt it could not afford a string of money-losing documentaries. So it tried something else.

SPONSOR RULES IN ABC DOCUS

By STEVE KNOLL

One of the major developments in broadcast journalism during the '60s has been the growth of ABC News from a skeletal operation to a worldwide news organization more or less competitive with NBC and CBS. Begun at the start of the decade by James C. Hagerty and carried forward by incumbent prexy Elmer W. Lower, the maturing of ABC News as a full-sized network news department has occurred in a remarkably short time.

Reflecting ABC prez Leonard Goldenson's commitment to parity with the other webs at any cost, the news buildup has constituted a serious drain for the hard-pressed network. Sacrifices of various kinds have been called for to hold down losses in the news area while keeping on a competitive keel with NBC and CBS. In order to remain a serious contender in the field of news documentaries while keeping the inevitable deficits from swelling out of control, ABC in recent years has maintained an extraordinary relationship with the Batten, Barton, Durstine & Osborn advertising agency and (via BBDO) with its principal documentary sponsors: Minnesota Mining &

Manufacturing, B. F. Goodrich and North American Rockwell.

As part of this unique relationship, the sponsors of ABC News documentaries have been able to select their subjects from among lists provided by ABC. They have been free to alter the concepts of documentaries from the ideas presented to them in ABC sales presentations, and have submitted their own ideas for documentaries which ABC has adopted. Moreover, after subjects have been selected, the documentary sponsors have kept in close touch during production, and at times have examined rough cuts and seen scripts. Further, the sponsor involvement has on occasion led to alteration of a program's content.

It is this unusual degree of sponsor and agency involvement which explains the rash of "cultural" and industrial-type ABC News documentaries about which numerous critics have commented during the past several seasons.

Fishing Trip—And the Catch

Part and parcel of this heretofore untold story is the tale of the annual summer excursion by ABC News execs to a midwest fishing lodge where, in

Variety, September 3, 1969, pp. 33, 48.   Reprinted by permission.   A response to this article by President Elmer V. Lower of ABC News appears in *Variety*, September 10, 1969, pp. 54, 89.

conference with sponsor representatives, the next season's
documentaries are selected. A
major role in this drama-in-real-
life is played by a BBDO exec
with the extraordinary title of
vice president and director of
news and public affairs, Loomis
C. Irish.

The process by which Min-
nesota Mining & Manufacturing
(3M) selects its documentaries
for the forthcoming season has
just been completed. The company bought a package of seven-
and-a-half hours of ABC news
documentaries, all but one hour
of which are scheduled for calendar 1970. The only news
documentaries ABC has planned
for 1970 so far are those in the
3M package. This fact alone
attests to 3M's major role in de-
termining the subjects to be
probed by ABC News. The
process of selection underlines
that key role, and 3M's continuing involvement afterwards rein-
forces it.

As happens every year, ABC
News submitted a list of some
30 proposed documentaries to
3M. Company exercised its
customary veto power, combing
through the titles and picking
the handful of projects it is
willing to bankroll. Production
will proceed on the latter, while
most or conceivably all of the
remainder will never go beyond
the stage of the ABC sales presentation to 3M.

This is what is known as
preselling documentaries, a practice in which the sponsor has
the last word on which subjects
and issues shall be explored
by tv documentary journalism.
Since most sponsors, 3M included, have shown an historical
aversion to controversial sub-

jects, the tendency on all networks in recent seasons has
been away from "hard" or issue-
oriented subject matter and toward the light or featurish items
which better conform with sponsor taste.

A major exception has been
when large corporate clients
bankroll documentaries reporting favorably on military or
space ventures in which those
companies are involved. Nevertheless, there remain a large
number of crucial domestic and
international concerns which
elude exploration apparently
because they are not the sponsor's cup of tea.

3M, ABC's only major news
documentary client at the moment, has no interest in doing
hard news documentaries. This
is reflected by the titles of the
shows 3M will sponsor during
calendar 1970: January—"The
Golden Age of the Automobile";
February—"The Westerners";
March—"The Unseen World";
April—"The Great Barrier Reef";
May—"Golden Age of the Railroad"; September 9—a repeat of
one of the above; also in September, "The Congo River."
"The Westerners," "The Great
Barrier Reef" and "The Congo
River" shows are tentative; pro-
ducers will first be sent into the
field to see whether there is
enough material to warrant programs on those subjects.

Three Without Sponsorship

With 3M firming up its plans
for the new season later than
usual this year, ABC in a rare
move scheduled three documentaries for the fall without
prior sponsor commitment and
outside the usual BBDO route.
As previously reported, these

three shows are issue-oriented: a Sept. 19 documentary on Congressional ethics, a study of inflation in November, and "Mission: Possible" (working title) on the challenges of the '70s, due in December. These three programs are rare exceptions to the general dictum at ABC News that production on documentaries during the regular season (September through May) cannot proceed unless sponsorship is assured in advance.

Armstrong Cork, sponsor of the Jacques Cousteau series, has renewed through 1970. Three Cousteau shows—one new and two repeats—are set for the fall. But B. F. Goodrich, which through BBDO had been a major ABC News documentary sponsor in seasons past, has bowed out. Goodrich had used the ABC docus for corporate advertising. Currently the principal thrust of Goodrich tv spending is in scatter plans for its tire division. North American Rockwell, which had entered tv via BBDO, has since changed agencies and its future in video is undetermined at this point. More about Rockwell anon.

Editorial Control

While the role of sponsors in picking ABC documentary subjects itself constitutes a form of censorship, the continuing sponsor and agency involvement afterwards is even more ominous. On this point sources close to the scene differ. Lester Cooper, exec producer of ABC News documentaries, maintains that "on any program, ABC News exercises total editorial control. This is unequivoc-

able." Thomas H. Wolf, veepee and director of television documentaries for ABC News, insists that "the sponsor has nothing whatsoever to do with a show once he buys it."

He adds, "During the past three years when I have been in charge of ABC News documentaries, we have never made any deletion, addition, revision or change in any documentary program at any time as a result of sponsor pressure—direct or indirect."

Sources at BBDO paint a somewhat different picture. While agreeing that supervision and control rests with ABC News, they point out that BBDO works closely with ABC in developing documentary ideas and is given progress reports during production. According to these sources, "We have certain things we do that no other agency is involved in. As a rule, we don't buy unless we know what we're buying. This situation is quite unique."

Close Relationship

These sources maintain that BBDO is involved with production, "does look at scripts and does see what is going on." Loomis Irish, BBDO's v.p. and director of news and public affairs, has a close working relationship with Tom Wolf, ABC News' documentary veep.

The ABC-BBDO alliance is seen as quite different from the relationship with NBC, where "they put on a news program . . . maybe they'll tell you what it's about, and you can either take it or leave it." These sources say that in most cases at ABC the sponsor sees the script. But they also maintain that keeping sponsor and agency informed does not necessarily mean giving them the right to make changes. As it's put, "Once the story line has been picked out, you have very little to say."

One instance in which a sponsor did have something to say was the case of "The Scientist," a documentary which aired on Nov. 29, 1968. The saga of "The Scientist" is part of the larger story of North American Rockwell's entry and exit from the field of ABC documentary sponsorship.

Rockwell Reneges

Early in 1968 BBDO had brought North American Rockwell into television. A sizable commitment to ABC News documentaries was envisioned. The initial agreement was for three programs with a couple of repeats, with the hope and expectation of a deeper Rockwell involvement in the future. Rockwell was to sponsor a series called "Man and His Universe," consisting of three programs: "The Scientist," "Cosmopolis" and "The View From Space." Actor George C. Scott was the narrator for the series.

"The Scientist," produced by Ernest Pendrell, dealt with the lives of three Harvard professors, including Nobel Prize-winning Dr. James D. Watson. With the assumption that North American Rockwell was in to stay, filming went ahead on "The Scientist," which was shot in February, 1968. At about that time, however, there had been a change in management at North American Rockwell. The new

advertising head at NAR reevaluated the tv commitment and decided he wanted out. This was after shooting had been completed on "The Scientist."

As a result, "The Scientist" sat on the shelf for some months while ABC tried with ultimate success to convince NAR to stay as sponsor. Rather than the start of a larger tv commitment as originally envisioned, the series of three shows with two repeats marked the sum total of Rockwell's involvement with ABC News docus.

An ABC News press release dated August 20, 1968, quoted H. Walton Cloke, veepee for public relations and advertising of North American Rockwell, as saying: "Since we are a new kind of corporation we felt a new medium—television—and a new kind of specials (sic) utilizing that medium, were the most effective and dramatic way to project North American Rockwell's corporate story." The release also quoted ABC News prexy Elmer Lower describing the NAR sponsorship as "indicative of an increasing trend of major corporations to recognize the importance of non-fiction television programming to their corporate identity."

Something New Is Added

There were several screenings of "The Scientist" for North American Rockwell not long before it finally aired in November, 1968. Although the show had been locked up, complete with George C. Scott's narration, the Rockwell representatives felt something should be added. They wanted clarification of Dr. Watson's project, which involved discovery of DNA, the master substance of heredity. And so, at two points in the program, an ABC staff announcer was spliced in the middle of actor Scott's narration, explaining Dr. Watson's project via voice-over. These changes disrupted continuity. Producer Pendrell was reportedly unhappy with them, although in response to an inquiry from VARIETY, he would say only that all aspects of the program were "decided by us here and done in the way we wanted."

(In Nielsen rankings of specials from September 11 (1968) through April 1 (1969), "The Scientist" was at the bottom of a list of 116 specs, pulling a 5.0 rating and 10 share.)

Sponsored Industrial

The third documentary in the "Man and His Universe" series was "The View From Space," which showed pictures of the moon taken by Apollo 8 and argued both visually and verbally for a continuation of the space program beyond the moon landing. Sponsor North American Rockwell built the Apollo spacecraft, and also boasts that it "has built more military aircraft than any other company." Throughout the Rockwell series, the line between commercial and program was a fine line indeed for the viewer to discern.

As Lower had stated, "Man and His Universe" did indeed represent an increasing trend by major corporations to use television documentaries to achieve their corporate objectives. According to ABC sources, the network "made a point" of not leading off the NAR series with "The View From Space" in order to allay any possible suspicion of a conflict of interest. It's doubtful, however, whether this objective was attained.

Of "The View From Space," critic Harriet Van Horne wrote: "Not surprisingly, the sponsor was a manufacturer of equipment essential to rocketing about in space. The commercials seemed to fill up half the program. And the nature of the sponsorship—in truth, an unvarnished bit of special pleading—seemed to be highly dubious."

"The View From Space" was promoted by newspaper advertisements placed by North American Rockwell.

An ABC News exec says "The View From Space" was "the closest we ever came" to a situation where "the sponsor was in the same line of business" as the documentary's subject. There have been other instances, however.

During 1966 and 1967 ABC aired three documentaries on the role of the Army and Air Force in Vietnam prepared with Pentagon cooperation. A fourth documentary, according to ABC's logs, was "comprised entirely of footage filmed under-fire by Marine photographers during World War II." Two of the programs were sponsored by 3M, and the other two by B. F. Goodrich. None contained any substantial criticism of the military, and all ignored the considerable controversy that was raging at the time regarding escalation of the war and the efficacy of the bombing of the North. The Air Force show was narrated by James Stewart, the Army show by Henry Fonda and the Marine show by Lee Marvin.

VARIETY's review of "War in the Skies," by *Mor.*, began: "It doesn't take a particularly suspicious mind to see a defense contractor's public relations gesture to armed services customers even when it's hidden behind the frail cover of a network news special. If B. F. Goodrich wants to buy an hour of tv to aimlessly extol the virtues of the Air Force, it should be properly identified. But putting the imprimatur of a network news department on a piece of puff demeans the web's news staff and the news business in general.

" 'War in the Skies' suffered even in comparison with a similar paean to the U.S. Marines courtesy of 3M a couple of months ago—also on ABC . . . " The reviewer charged ABC with "a total suspension of critical news evaluation, a lack of spot news value, and a void in the area of insight into the subject."

Among many other services to the military, Goodrich manufactures the wheels and brakes for the Lockheed C5A plane used by the Air Force.

In the case of "Our Time in Hell," the Marine documentary, the VARIETY reviewer wrote, "There are compelling reasons for doubting that this show sprang from any historical or artistic imperative at ABC-TV, and the show raises serious questions about the ambiguities of the relationship between a company holding defense contracts and a branch of the Armed Forces, in this case the U.S. Marine Corps. Aside from several external factors, the lack of historical art in the film strongly suggests that this was less a documentary and more an hour-long public relations plug for the Marines paid for by 3M—and ultimately by the taxpayers through defense contracts."

It is common for shows sponsored by B. F. Goodrich and 3M to be screened by the sponsor in advance of airing. In one case not considered unusual—a program called "Who in '68?," which aired Aug. 17, 1967— B. F. Goodrich was shown a rough cut. In that instance, no changes were requested by the sponsor. However, Goodrich has not always been so mute.

6 Source Control

In the early 1960s, Rafael Trujillo, dictator of the Dominican Republic, hired a New York press agent named Harry Klemfuss, to help build pro-Trujillo sentiment in this country. Klemfuss, in turn, hired the U.S. Press Association, Inc., a company specializing in canned news and editorials. For a fee of only $125, the company mailed the following "news item" to 1,300 dailies and weeklies throughout the country: "Today the Dominican Republic . . . is a bulwark of strength against Communism and has been widely cited as one of the cleanest, healthiest, happiest countries on the globe. Guiding spirit of this fabulous transformation is Generalissimo Trujillo. . . ." It is not known how many papers actually carried the story, but Klemfuss and Trujillo considered their money well spent.

Only a small percentage of the news covered by the mass media comes from on-the-scene reporting. The vast majority must be obtained from news sources—and from public relations men like Harry Klemfuss. Sources and their P.R. men are seldom unbiased. In one way or another they inevitably try to control the form and content of the news. Such news management on the part of both government and private sources has a mammoth effect on the nature of the news reaching the public.

Many techniques are available for managing the news. One peren-
nial favorite is the junket; after a free trip to the finest resorts of Spain,
a travel editor may feel honor-bound to say only nice things. Canned
news and editorials are often effective, especially with small newspapers desperate for filler. Conventions, demonstrations, stunts, and
the like are irresistible to reporters and are ideal for popularizing anything from a political ideology to a new detergent.

By far the most important vehicle for news management is the press
release. In a single ten-day period, one small country newspaper in
Vermont received 149 handouts from sixty-eight different sources, to-
taling to 950 pages or nearly a quarter of a million words. The list included eighty releases from businesses; sixteen from philanthropic
organizations; fourteen from government; six from lobbies and pressure
groups; twenty-nine from educational institutions; and four from political
parties. And that was a small newspaper. The average metropolitan
daily receives well over a hundred releases a day. Roughly half the
news printed in America's newspapers starts with a press release.

News managers spend most of their time trying to get some item into
the news; the rest of it they spend trying to keep some item out of the
news. As a rule, they have better luck at the first task than at the second. American journalism has a long tradition of fighting secrecy—
especially government secrecy—with all the resources at its command.
To be sure, there are still plenty of secrets in government, and it is by
no means unheard-of for a private corporation to blackout a piece of
embarrassing news through subtle bribes or threats. But for every story
the news managers succeed in killing, there are scores of stories they
manage to inspire or plant.

Government secrecy is hardest to cope with when it revolves around
the issue of national security. In 1961, the **New York Times** discovered
that the CIA was secretly preparing anti-Castro forces for an invasion of
Cuba. After considerable debate, the paper decided to downplay the
story. The invasion turned out to be a fiasco. President Kennedy later
admitted that it might have been better for the country if the **Times**
had run the full story. Yet only a year later, at the time of the Cuban
missile crisis, Kennedy personally asked the **Times** to keep the crisis
secret while he negotiated with the Soviet Union. The **Times** agreed,
and the negotiations were a triumph for American diplomacy.

Government secrecy and news management reached their height
during the war in Vietnam. Wartime policy and the conduct of the
war itself were hidden from the public through misleading public
statements, frequent censorship, and even outright lies. The resulting
"credibility gap" was dramatically documented in a top secret government report on the war, the so-called "Pentagon Papers." In 1971, a

former Defense Department consultant gave the **New York Times** an unauthorized copy of this report.   The **Times** decided to publish long excerpts from it.   The government immediately obtained an injunction
forbidding publication.   In an unusually confused decision (each Justice
wrote his own opinion), the Supreme Court granted the **Times** the right
to publish the report.

The significance of the Pentagon Papers is twofold.   On the one
hand, the report disclosed government news management at its most
dangerous.   On the other hand, the report resulted in an even more
serious attempt at news management—an attempt which the Supreme
Court refused to countenance.

In the selections that follow, the **Times** editorializes on its reasons for
publishing the Pentagon Papers, while Supreme Court Justices Hugo
Black and Warren Burger disagree on the legality of such publication.

The Pentagon Papers
and the New York Times

The Vietnam Papers

On Nov. 25, 1964, some three weeks after President Johnson's election,
the *Times* observed editorially that "another Vietnam reassessment is under way . . . [and] if there is to be a new policy now, if an Asian war is
to be converted into an American war, the country has a right to insist
that it be told what has changed so profoundly in the last two months to
justify it."   The country was not told.

Six months later, after repeated demands for "a straightforward ex-
planation" of what was clearly becoming a major land war on the continent of Asia, this newspaper noted that "there is still no official explana-
tion offered for a move that fundamentally alters the character of the
American involvement in Vietnam" and pleaded "for the President to
take the country into his confidence. . . ."

These comments illustrate how Congress and the American people were kept in the dark about fundamental policy decisions affecting the very life of this democracy during the most critical period of the war. The conviction even then that the Government was not being frank with the American people has been fully confirmed by the massive Pentagon history and documentation which the *Times* began to publish last week —until the Government undertook to censor it.

The running commentary and documents that did appear in this newspaper before the Government moved to block them throw a clear spotlight on the decision-making process during the period up to and including the major escalation of the Vietnam War in 1964 and 1965. The multi-volume study on which the *Times'* account was based shows beyond cavil how the decisions affecting American participation in and conduct of the war were planned and executed while their far-reaching political effect and profound significance, fully appreciated at the top reaches of government, were either deliberately distorted or withheld altogether from the public.

Even more important, the papers as published thus far suggest that almost no one in the upper ranks of the Administration during this crucial period six and seven years ago was probing into the basic political issue on which the military operation depended: Was the Saigon Government's control of South Vietnam of such vital, long-range interest to the United States that it warranted an open-ended American military involvement—or was this really an unexamined conclusion that had already become an article of faith? Nearly every official concerned was discussing the tactics and strategy of the war, how to handle it, how to win it, how to come out of it, what plans to make under various contingencies. These were important matters indeed and the officials in question would not have been doing their duty if they had failed to consider them. They should not be faulted for this; nor was it in any way improper to have planned for every conceivable military eventuality.

But the missing factor was discussion or argumentation over the *raison d'être* of the war and the rationale for continuing massive American involvement in it. It seems to have been accepted without question by virtually everyone in the top ranks, except Under Secretary of State George Ball, that the interests of the United States did indeed lie, at almost any cost and overriding almost any risk, in military victory for the South Vietnamese Government even to the point of major American participation in a war on the land mass of Southeast Asia.

This was the premise, this the context, and this the fateful error. If, as the principal officers of the Government saw the country being drawn into such a war, a full and frank debate and discussion in Congress and outside had been undertaken, it is quite possible that events would have moved in a different way. No one will ever know, for this "open covenant, openly arrived at" between American Government and American people never materialized.

This, then, is what the Vietnam Papers prove—not venality, not evil motivation, but rather an arrogant disregard for the Congress, for the public and for the inherent obligation of the responsibilities of leadership in a democratic society. The papers are not only part of the historical record; they are an essential part of that record. They are highly classified documents and so is the analytical study on which the *Times* running commentary was based. But they carry the story of Vietnam no farther than 1968—now three years ago; they in no way affect current plans, operations or policy; and there seems no longer any justification for these papers—along with many others in governmental files—to bear the kind of classification that keeps them from general public access. Overclassification and misclassification of documents is at best a normal reflection of governmental inertia; but, as here, it is often used to conceal governmental error.

The material was not published by the *Times* for purposes of recrimination or to establish scapegoats or to heap blame on any individual in civilian or military ranks. It was published because the American public has a right to have it and because, when it came into the hands of the *Times*, it was its function as a free and uncensored medium of information to make it public. This same principle held for the *Washington Post* when it too obtained some of the papers. To have acted otherwise would have been to default on a newspaper's basic obligation to the American people under the First Amendment, which is precisely the point that Federal District Judge Murray Gurfein suggested in his memorable decision in this newspaper's favor last Saturday.

And yet the Government of the United States, in an action unprecedented in modern American history, sought and is continuing to seek to silence both the *New York Times* and the *Washington Post*, claiming that "irreparable injury" to the national security would be caused by publication of further chapters in the Vietnam study. The fact is that "irreparable injury" has been done to the Government itself, not because of anything that has been published but, quite the contrary, because of the extraordinary action the Government took to thwart and subvert in this manner the constitutional principle of freedom of the press which is the very essence of American democracy. Judge Gurfein's decision—whether or not it is sustained on appeal—surely represents a landmark in the endless struggle of free men and free institutions against the unwarranted exercise of governmental authority.

U.S. v. New York Times *and* Washington Post
(*403 U.S. 713, 1971*)

MR. JUSTICE BLACK, *with whom* MR. JUSTICE DOUGLAS *joins, concurring.*

I adhere to the view that the Government's case against the *Washington Post* should have been dismissed and that the injunction against the *New York Times* should have been vacated without oral argument when the cases were first presented to this Court. I believe that every moment's continuance of the injunctions against these newspapers amounts to a flagrant, indefensible and continuing violation of the First Amendment. Furthermore, after oral arguments, I agree completely that we must affirm the judgment of the Court of Appeals for the District of Columbia and reverse the judgment of the Court of Appeals for the Second Circuit for the reasons stated by my brothers Douglas and Brennan. In my view it is unfortunate that some of my brethren are apparently willing to hold that the publication of news may sometimes be enjoined. Such a holding would make a shambles of the First Amendment.

Our Government was launched in 1789 with the adoption of the Constitution. The Bill of Rights, including the First Amendment, followed in 1791. Now, for the first time in the 182 years since the founding of the Republic, the Federal courts are asked to hold that the First Amendment does not mean what it says, but rather means that the Government can halt the publication of current news of vital importance to the people of this country.

In seeking injunctions against these newspapers and in its presentation to the court, the executive branch seems to have forgotten the essential purpose and history of the First Amendment. When the Constitution was adopted, many people strongly opposed it because the document contained no bill of rights to safeguard certain basic freedoms. They especially feared that the new powers granted to a central government might be interpreted to permit the government to curtail freedom of religion, press, assembly and speech. In response to an overwhelming public clamor, James Madison offered a series of amendments to satisfy citizens that these great liberties would remain safe and beyond the power of government to abridge. Madison proposed what later became the First Amendment in three parts, two of which are set out below, and one of which proclaimed: "The people shall not be deprived or abridged of their right to speak, to write, or to publish their sentiments; and the freedom of the press, as one of the great bulwarks of liberty, shall be inviolable." The amendments were offered to curtail and restrict the general powers granted to the executive, legislative and judicial branches two years before in the original Constitution. The Bill of Rights changed the original Constitution into a new charter under which no branch of government could abridge the people's freedoms of press, speech, religion and assembly.

Yet the Solicitor General argues and some members of the Court appear to agree that the general powers of the Government adopted in the original Constitution should be interpreted to limit and restrict the specific and emphatic guarantees of the Bill of Rights adopted later. I can imagine no greater perversion of history. Madison and the other framers of the First Amendment, able men that they were, wrote in language they earnestly believed could never be misunderstood: "Congress shall make no law . . . abridging the freedom of the press." Both the history and language of the First Amendment support the view that the press must be left free to publish news, whatever the source, without censorship, injunctions or prior restraints.

In the First Amendment the Founding Fathers gave the free press the protection it must have to fulfill its essential role in our democracy. The press was to serve the governed, not the governors. The Government's power to censor the press was abolished so that the press would remain forever free to censure the Government. The press was protected so that it could bare the secrets of government and inform the people./ Only a free and unrestrained press can effectively expose deception in government. And paramount among the responsibilities of a free press is the duty to prevent any part of the Government from deceiving the people and sending them off to distant lands to die of foreign fevers and foreign shot and shell. In my view, far from deserving condemnation for their courageous reporting, the *New York Times*, the *Washington Post* and other newspapers should be commended for serving the purpose that the Founding Fathers saw so clearly. In revealing the workings of government that led to the Vietnam war, the newspapers nobly did precisely that which the founders hoped and trusted they would do.

The Government's case here is based on premises entirely different from those that guided the framers of the First Amendment. The Solicitor General has carefully and emphatically stated:

"Now, Mr. Justice [Black], your construction of . . . [the First Amendment] is well known, and I certainly respect it. You say that no law means no law, and that should be obvious. I can only say, Mr. Justice, that to me it is equally obvious that 'no law,' and I would seek to persuade the Court that that is true . . . [t]here are other parts of the Constitution that grant power and responsibilities to the executive end . . . the First Amendment was not intended to make it impossible for the executive to function or to protect the security of the United States."

And the Government argues in its brief that in spite of the First Amendment, "the authority of the executive department to protect the nation against publication of information whose disclosure would endanger the national security stems from two interrelated sources: The constitutional power of the President over the conduct of foreign affairs and his authority as Commander in Chief."

In other words, we are asked to hold that despite the First Amendment's emphatic command, the executive branch, the Congress and the judiciary can make laws enjoining publication of current news and abridging freedom of the press in the name of "national security." The Government does not even attempt to rely on act of Congress. Instead it makes the bold and dangerously far-reaching contention that the courts should take it upon themselves to "make" a law abridging freedom of the press in the name of equity, Presidential power and national security, even when the representatives of the people in Congress have adhered to the command of the First Amendment and refused to make such a law. . . .

To find that the President has "inherent power" to halt the publication of news by resort to the courts would wipe out the First Amendment and destroy the fundamental liberty and security of the very people the Government hopes to make "secure." No one can read the history of the adoption of the First Amendment without being convinced beyond any doubt that it was injunctions like those sought here that Madison and his collaborators intended to outlaw in this nation for all time.

The word "security" is a broad, vague generality whose contours should not be invoked to abrogate the fundamental law embodied in the First Amendment. The guarding of military and diplomatic secrets at the expense of informed representative government provides no real security for our Republic.

The framers of the First Amendment, fully aware of both the need to defend a new nation and the abuses of the English and colonial Governments, sought to give this new society strength and security by providing that freedom of speech, press, religion and assembly should not be abridged. This thought was eloquently expressed in 1937 by Mr. Chief Justice Hughes—great man and great Chief Justice that he was— when the Court held a man could not be punished for attending a meeting run by Communists.

"The greater the importance of safeguarding the community from incitements to the overthrow of our institutions by force and violence, the more imperative is the need to preserve inviolate the constitutional rights of free speech, free press and free assembly in order to maintain the opportunity for free political discussion, to the end that government may be responsive to the will of the people and that changes, if desired, may be obtained by peaceful means. Therein lies the security of the Republic, the very foundation of constitutional government."

MR. CHIEF JUSTICE BURGER, *dissenting.*

So clear are the constitutional limitations on prior restraint against expression, that from the time of Near v. Minnesota, 283 U.S. 697 (1931), until recently in Organization for a Better Austin v. Keefe (1971), we have had little occasion to be concerned with cases involving prior restraints against news reporting on matters of public interest. There is, therefore, little variation among the members of the Court in terms of resistance to prior restraints against publication. Adherence of this basic constitutional principle, however, does not make this case a simple one. In this case, the imperative of a free and unfettered press comes into collision with another imperative, the effective functioning of a complex modern government, and specifically the effective exercise of certain constitutional powers of the executive. Only those who view the First Amendment as an absolute in all circumstances—a view I respect, but reject—can find such a case as this to be simple or easy.

This case is not simple for another and more immediate reason. We do not know the facts of the case. No District Judge knew all the facts. No Court of Appeals Judge knew all the facts. No member of this Court knows all the facts.

Why are we in this posture, in which only those judges to whom the First Amendment is absolute and permits of no restraint in any circumstances or for any reason, are really in a position to act?

I suggest we are in this posture because these cases have been conducted in unseemly haste. Mr. Justice Harlan covers the chronology of events demonstrating the hectic pressures under which these cases have been processed and I need not restate them. The prompt setting of these cases reflects our universal abhorrence of prior restraint. But prompt judicial action does not mean unjudicial haste.

Here, moreover, the frenetic haste is due in large part to the manner in which the *Times* proceeded from the date it obtained the purloined documents. It seems reasonably clear now that the haste precluded reasonable and deliberate judicial treatment of these cases and was not warranted. The precipitous action of this court aborting a trial not yet completed is not the kind of judicial conduct which ought to attend the disposition of a great issue.

The newspapers make a derivative claim under the First Amendment: they denominate this right as the public right to know; by implication, the *Times* asserts a sole trusteeship of that right by virtue of its journalistic "scoop." The right is asserted as an absolute. Of course, the First Amendment right itself is not an absolute, as Justice Holmes so long ago pointed out in his aphorism concerning the right to shout of fire in a crowded theater. There are other exceptions, some of which Chief Justice Hughes mentioned by way of example in Near v. Minnesota. There are no doubt other exceptions no one has had occasion to describe or discuss. Conceivably such exceptions may be lurking in these cases and would have been flushed had they been properly considered in the trial courts, free from unwarranted deadlines and frenetic pressures.

A great issue of this kind should be tried in a judicial atmosphere conducive to thoughtful, reflective deliberation, especially when haste, in terms of hours, is unwarranted in light of the long period the *Times,* by its own choice, deferred publication.

It is not disputed that the *Times* has had unauthorized possession of the documents for three to four months, during which it has had its expert analysts studying them, presumably digesting them and preparing the material for publication. During all of this time, the *Times,* presumably in its capacity as trustee of the public's "right to know," has held up publication for purposes it considered proper and thus public knowledge was delayed. No doubt this was for a good reason; the analysis of 7,000 pages of complex material drawn from a vastly greater volume of material would inevitably take time and the writing of good news stories takes time.

But why should the United States Government, from whom this information was illegally acquired by someone, along with all the counsel, trial judges, and appellate judges be placed under needless pressure? After these months of deferral, the alleged right to know has somehow and suddenly become a right that must be vindicated instanter [instantly].

Would it have been unreasonable, since the newspaper could anticipate the Government's objections to release of secret material, to give the Government an opportunity to review the entire collection and determine whether agreement could be reached on publication? Stolen or not, if security was not in fact jeopardized, much of the material could no doubt have been declassified, since it spans a period ending in 1968.

With such an approach—one that great newspapers have in the past practiced and stated editorially to be the duty of honorable press—the newspapers and Government might well have narrowed the area of disagreement as to what was and was not publishable, leaving the remainder to be resolved in orderly litigation if necessary. To me it is hardly believable that a newspaper long regarded as a great institution in American life would fail to perform one of the basic and simple duties of every citizen with respect to the discovery or possession of stolen property or secret Government documents. That duty, I had thought— perhaps naively—was to report forthwith, to responsible public officers.

This duty rests on taxi drivers, justices and the *New York Times.* The course followed by the *Times,* whether so calculated or not, removed any possibility of orderly litigation of the issues. If the action of the judges up to now has been correct, that result is sheer happenstance.

Our grant of the writ before final judgment in the *Times* case aborted the trial in the District Court before it had made a complete record pursuant to the mandate of the Court of Appeals, Second Circuit.

The consequences of all this melancholy series of events is that we literally do not know what we are acting on. As I see it we have been forced to deal with litigation concerning rights of great magnitude without an adequate record, and surely without time for adequate treatment either in the prior proceedings or in this court. It is interesting to note that counsel in oral argument before this Court were frequently unable to respond to questions on factual points. Not surprisingly they pointed out that they had been working literally "around the clock" and simply were unable to review the documents that give rise to these cases and were not familiar with them. This Court is in no better posture. I agree with Mr. Justice Harlan and Mr. Justice Blackmun but I am not prepared to reach the merits.

I would affirm the Court of Appeals for the Second Circuit and allow the District Court to complete the trial aborted by our grant of certiorari, meanwhile preserving the status quo in the *Post* case. I would direct that the District Court on remand give priority to the *Times* case to the exclusion of all other business of that court but I would not set arbitrary deadlines.

I should add that I am in general agreement with much of what Mr. Justice White has expressed with respect to penal sanctions concerning communication or retention of documents or information relating to the national defense.

We all crave speedier judicial processes, but when judges are pressured as in these cases the result is a parody of the judicial process.

7 Government Control

The First Amendment to the U.S. Constitution reads in part: "Congress shall make no law . . . abridging the freedom of speech or of the press." This is the earliest and most important statement of the theoretical relationship between the American government and the mass media —independence.

The libertarian theory, which the First Amendment embodies, holds that the government should exercise no control whatever over the content of the media. It is by no means the only theory around. The authoritarian theory, for example, permits the state to prohibit those media actions it deems undesirable. The Soviet theory goes further, allowing the government to prescribe what the media should do as well as what they should avoid. And the social responsibility theory leaves it to the experts to set standards for the media, with the state enforcing those standards only when absolutely necessary.

Despite the First Amendment, the practical relationship between the government and the media in the United States is a mixture of the libertarian, authoritarian, and social responsibility theories. Consider, for example, the following direct government controls over media content:

- Copyright law, designed to protect the rights of authors and publishers.
- Obscenity law, designed to protect the morals of the audience and the nation.
- Libel law, designed to protect the reputations of news makers and sources.
- Privacy law, designed to protect the privacy of individual citizens.
- Advertising law, designed to protect the public against fraud and misrepresentation.
- Sedition law, designed to protect the government itself.

Most if not all of these regulations are sane, sound, and sensible. Nevertheless, they do restrict the freedom of the mass media. They are not strictly consistent with the libertarian theory. And as Justice Hugo Black of the Supreme Court has pointed out from time to time, they are not strictly consistent with the First Amendment.

The government controls the mass media in indirect ways as well. Official secrecy and news management diminish the reporter's access to news. Demands that newsmen reveal their sources to government investigators make it more difficult to obtain controversial interviews. Antitrust actions limit the scope of media monopolists. Even the second-class mailing permit, a great boon to all publishers, is conditional upon acceptance of certain government-imposed regulations.

The power of the government to regulate the print media is next to nothing compared to its power over broadcasting. Space on the broadcast spectrum is limited; there are more applicants for radio and TV stations than there are channels and frequencies to go around. The Federal Communications Commission, a government agency, is therefore empowered to license all broadcasters in the country. It is the FCC that decides who gets the license—and who keeps it.

In theory, the FCC may revoke the license of any broadcaster who has failed to operate in the public interest. In practice, the Commission is reluctant to utilize this power; it has taken away barely a dozen licenses in the past forty years. It tends to ignore the sins of individual station owners and concentrates instead on regulating the industry as a whole.

The fairness doctrine, for example, requires broadcasters to present both sides of controversial issues. The duopoly rule limits the number of stations a single company may own. The obscenity provision forbids indecent language over the air. Other regulations deal with the technical specifications for broadcast transmitters. Still others are designed to encourage the growth of FM radio, cable television, and the like. It is quite possible for a station to obey every one of these regulations and still do a poor job of serving the public.   Such a station is unlikely to have any trouble with the FCC.

In November of 1967, WBBM-TV in Chicago broadcast what purported to be a university pot party.   Many observers in and out of government objected to the broadcast.   Both Congress and the FCC conducted zealous investigations.   In the end no action was taken—but the uproar frightened many broadcasters and possibly deterred them from planning other controversial documentaries.

This is typical of government control over the mass media.   The government meddles a lot, far more than the libertarian theory would allow.   Its jawboning tactics force the media to be cautious about controversy.   But in the end it seldom takes any action.

The Government versus WBBM–TV

FCC DELAYS PROBE OF
WBBM–TV'S "POT" SHOW

Washington, May 7—At the request of the House Investigations Subcommittee, the FCC last week postponed by six weeks its probe into a program broadcast by WBBM-TV in Chicago involving marijuana smoking.

The Commission set the hearing for May 14, as there had been charges that the CBS o&o directly or indirectly helped stage the pot party that was the subject of its documentary. The session is now scheduled for June 25, as the investigations subcommittee headed by Rep. Harley Staggers (D-W. Va.) is conducting its own probe of the program.

—May 8, 1968, p. 223.

TV'S "POT PARTY" HANGOVER

HEARINGS RAISE RAFT OF ISSUES

Washington, May 21.—A Greek myth speaks of a many-headed monster, Hydra, whose heads grow back faster than they can be chopped off. Hy- dra seemed to be reincarnated in abstract as the House Investigations Subcommittee grappled with the many-headed controversies involved in the show "Pot

All the articles in this selection are reprinted by permission from *Variety*.   Complete citations are located after each article.

Party At A University," which CBS o&o WBBM-TV in Chicago aired last November. Here is a thumbnail sketch of the issues touched on at the hearing:

1.) Are there circumstances in which an investigative reporter can witness a crime and make journalistic use of it without reporting it to the police? Where should the line be drawn?

2.) Even granting the above for a newspaper reporter, what about a broadcast journalist? Should the FCC allow a pubic interest license to rest with a station that will broadcast a crime without reporting it?

3.) Isn't there a basic insoluble paradox in the FCC requiring a licensee to be fully responsible for what is aired, and at the same time encouraging local programming and allowing absentee ownership?

4.) What is the relationship between a network o&o and the corporation and what should it be? Can Dr. Frank Stanton be president of a firm that owns a station and still be unaware of what local documentaries it has carried until an after-the-fact controversy has brought it to his attention?

On a more concrete scale, there are these questions to be resolved:

1.) Did WBBM-TV reporter Jack Missett in any way stage the party at which marijuana was smoked?

2.) Did the station do a responsible job of checking the accuracy of the show and of Missett's reporting?

3.) Was Missett reasonably discreet in buying a "nickel bag" of pot, he says, because he feared physical violence (he immediately threw the pot out)?

4.) Was the show really filmed on the Northwestern U. campus? How does one define "campus"?

5.) Does WBBM-TV really destroy all extraneous documentary footage within a couple of days? Should stations be required to keep such footage on file?

6.) Was the FCC lax in questioning station employees who knew Missett bought marijuana (they didn't say because the FCC didn't ask)?

7.) Did the FCC try to intimidate subcommittee witness or witnesses?

8.) Did WBBM-TV air the show just to hypo ratings at the start of a rating period? Was that why a special American Research Bureau survey was run on the show?

9.) Did Missett represent WBBM-TV as wishing to air a sympathetic view of pot smoking in an effort to loosen the law? Was that the station management's intention?

10.) What substance is there to the character jibes of CBS veep-station manager Edward Kenefick against a Northwestern official (a nervous chain-smoker who allegedly claimed the station was being used by a "Communist conspiracy") and of Missett against a central witness ("erratic" and "untrustworthy")?

11.) Finally, an issue not mentioned so far, but sure to come up when the FCC visits the subcommittee: Just why is the subcommittee interrupting the commission's own announced inquiry into the program before it even has had a chance to hold a public hearing, as planned, in Chicago?

—May 22, 1968, p. 35.

A "RELUCTANT" FCC OPENS HEARINGS
IN CHICAGO ON WBBM-TV'S "POT PARTY"

BY MORRY ROTH

Chicago, Oct. 8.—WBBM-TV, the Chi CBS o&o, today (Tues.) begins another episode in what amounts to a giant hangover resulting from a "pot party" special aired Nov. 1, 2 and 3 of last year. Having been worked over thoroughly in May by Rep. Harley O. Staggers' Special Subcommittee on Investigations of the House Commerce Committee, the station and web must now face a FCC task force headed by chief hearing examiner James Cunningham.

No one is quite certain what to expect from the estimated five days of Windy City hearings, and there is considerable uncertainty as to what the commission is investigating.

The transcript of the earlier subcommittee hearings clearly indicates that FCC field investigators had looked into the matter shortly after it happened and decided to take no action at that time. The Chi hearings were called only after the Staggers subcommittee hauled the CBS brass down to Washington for a going over, and it is largely felt here that the commission has unwillingly been dragged into an investigation that it considers treacherous in terms of program control.

Few were more astonished at the monumental flap over the three-part show, entitled "Pot Party At a University," than was WBBM-TV itself. The subject had been kicked around in the Chicago newspapers and the university press in the area for some time prior to the show. The show itself was pitched at a low emotional level and was liberally salted with anti-marijuana experts.

Fund-raising Slant

What WBBM-TV apparently did not anticipate was the intensity of the response of Northwestern Univ., on whose campus the party was filmed. Known as a staid and conservative educational institution, Northwestern was at the time in the midst of a major fund-raising drive and was specifically involved in soliciting a major gift from one donor who had earlier shown a dislike of student activism and a lessening of university discipline in personal matters. According to the May hearings, a university representative alternately pleaded with and threatened the station early on the day the show was to be aired.

The Staggers subcommittee found several things to its dislike in the station's handling of the show. It implied that the station put an inordinate advertising budget behind the show, which the station denies. Nor did the subcommittee like the fact that WBBM-TV screened the show for Chicago Daily News tv editor Dean Gysel prior to its showing. The subcommittee also found it ominous that WBBM-TV veepeeg.m. Ed Kenefick ordered an overnight ARB rating on the day after the first seg. Kenefick replied that the screenings were not unusual and he called for the overnight only after the brouhaha.

Denial of "Rig"

On subsidiary arguments, the station has denied that it arranged for or "rigged" the party at which eight students and non-students smoked marijuana. As to whether the station should have reported the pot party as a crime to the police, it maintains that there is sufficient news tradition to the contrary and that such action would inhibit newsgathering on social ills.

(Under Illinois law, possession of marijuana is a crime punishable by imprisonment for two to 10 years for a first offense and up to life imprisonment for repeaters. Inducing others to possess or use marijuana is punishable up to 25 years' imprisonment. It is also a Federal offense. No charges have been placed against the station, although the State's Attorney has looked into the case.)

The House subcommittee said that it was looking into the case to ascertain whether WBBM-TV violated the Communications Act of 1934, as amended, and/or violated the Federal Trade Commission Act. It also sought to determine if each of these commissions adequately administered the provisions in their "organic statutes" which pertain to facts and circumstances involved, and finally asked if the pertinent statutes and regulations contain provisions with adequate safeguards to protect the public interest. As in the May hearings, the Chi defense of the station will be handled by Newton Minow, former FCC head now in private law practice.

Chi broadcaster sentiment is nearly unanimously behind WBBM-TV. It is felt that the station has been caught in what is considered a growing breach between Staggers and the FCC. Or as one station (not WBBM) exec put it: "Staggers is getting tired of looking over the FCC's shoulder and now wants to climb up on their back."

—October 9, 1968, pp. 35, 49.

HOW WBBM-TV'S "POT PARTY"
WAS BORN

BY MORRY ROTH

Chicago, Oct. 15.—Against the burning issues in the FCC Chicago hearings into two (Nov. 1–2) 1967 inserts in WBBM-TV's 10 p.m. newscasts entitled "Pot Party At A University," the chronology of events has unrolled with little contest.

In August of last year, WBBM-TV news director Bob Ferrante and g.m. Ed Kenefick began discussing newspaper revelations of the increase in marijuana usage by upper middle class youths, particularly at Chi-area universities. Ferrante mentioned this interest to John Missett, a young reporter who had come to the station as a broadcast intern from Northwestern U. Missett told Ferrante that he would nose about the university, and shortly thereafter, he reported back that there was considerable pot smoking there and at other nearby universities.

A Witness Is Born

Missett contacted a graduate student at the university who said he would help them get information on pot usage. However, the grad student insisted on a promise of a panel type show and Missett, after checking with his superiors, said this could not be done. The grad student later turned up as a hostile witness at Commerce Subcommittee hearings in Washington in May of this year.

In early October, Missett made a new contact who said that he would look for a pot party that Missett might attend. He called back a few days later that such a party was to take place. It was originally set to be held in Chicago near the university, but the owner of the apartment backed off and it was reset for a private rooming house in the Northwestern complex in neighboring Evanston, Ill.

(The location of the "party" became a matter of considerable contention. The FCC maintains that the show implied that the pot party was on university property. WBBM-TV counsel Newton Minow produced a Northwestern catalog which showed the private rooming house to be in an area shaded to indicate it was on the campus.)

Life of the Party

According to Missett, his first intent was to attend the party and then to give a first-hand report of it on the show. He did suggest that he would like to film the party, and was surprised when the bid was accepted. Missett cleared the bid with Ferrante, and a camera crew was assigned to accompany the reporter at the Oct. 22 party. Missett promised to protect the identity of the participants.

The filming of the party was routine. However, when it was over, one of the participants asked Missett for some money. Missett refused and the participant became insistent, protesting that the party-goers "had the munchies" (post-pot hunger) and needed the money for sandwiches. After considerable badgering, according to Missett, he agreed to purchase a "nickle bag" ($5 worth). The spokesman for the group poured some pot into a paper cup and placed it on the table. Missett put $5 on the table, picked up the marijuana, walked to a nearby stairwell and threw it away. In the earlier investigation, Missett admitted to acquiring the pot, but did not tell his superiors about the money, per an agreement with the participants that he would not divulge anything that took place off camera. Apparently one of the guests told investigators about the buy, and Missett admitted the purchase in a supplementary statement.

On the Friday (Oct. 27) preceding the broadcast, Ferrante called the show to the attention of WBBM-TV ad-pub director Bruce Bloom, and Bloom wrote copy for an ad and had artwork prepared. The original title of the show in the ads was "Pot Party At Northwestern University." However, when the ad was shown to Kenefick, he said that the program was about the general university usage of marijuana and had it retitled "Pot Party At A University."

When the ads broke on the day of the show, Northwestern, already aware of the filming, became upset. The University's public relations director called to say that the station should have consulted with him first. Later the same day, Northwestern's director of development, Franklin Kreml, visited Kenefick in an attempt to get the show stopped.

Among other allegations, Kreml said that pot usage was part of a Communist conspiracy to embarrass the university. Kenefick asked for proof, and Kreml said that it would require "$50,000 and six months." Kenefick offered the university equal time, an offer that was never accepted.

The show was aired in two segments on the Nov. 1 and 2 newscasts at 10 p.m. It contained filmed statements from a representative of the Federal Narcotics Bureau and a doctor, both of whom warned of the dangers of using marijuana.

—October 16, 1968, pp. 38, 76.

"POT PARTY" ISSUE DESTRUCTIVE TO INVESTIGATIVE NEWS, CHI B'CASTERS SAY

Chicago, Oct. 15.—As the FCC ground through the first week of its field hearings into the propriety of WBBM-TV's Nov. 1967 airing of a special on the use of marijuana at Northwestern University, it became increasingly clear that the Chi legalistics are a road company version of the May '68 Commerce Subcommittee hearings in Washington, and that FCC counsel Joseph Stirmer is using the Subcommittee transcript as his script with minor variations.

Stirmer has meticulously been tracking witnesses through the shoals of previous testimony in the apparent hope of catching someone in a contradiction. The technique is at a minimum tedious for anyone familiar with the Capitol hearings earlier this year, although the Chi newspapers have not been reluctant to rub salt in the broadcast wound when the testimony rises above the routine.

Bureaucratic Crossfire

With at least one more week of hearings to take place in the new Federal courtroom, there is abundant evidence in the handling of the hearings that the Windy City investigation is a small skirmish in a larger battle going on between the Commission and Congress, and specifically Rep. Harley Stagger's House Committee on Interstate and Foreign Commerce.

At this juncture, the CBS-owned station appears less concerned that any new damaging evidence will pop up (although this is still a possibility), but is troubled by what will happen to the testimony when it is taken back to Washington. The prime question is whether the FCC is just going through the motions to satisfy the Subcommittee or whether it will crack down hard to show Congress that it is doing its job. In this regard, WBBM-TV is a bystander, innocent or not, in the bureaucratic crossfire.

"We've Done No Wrong"

A CBS source said that the web insists that it has done no wrong and would not accept even a mild rebuke as a compromise. The station's license renewal was due last December and has been held up pending the investigation. One possible "deal" would be for the Commission to grant a two-year license this December and consider the past year to be "time served."

After four days of hearings, WBBM-TV appears to be unshaken in its factual representation. The points of dispute so far have been matters of interpretation and intent. For instance, was the station trying to hypo ratings in the tight 10 p.m. news race or was it actually performing a public service in bringing to light a criti-

cal social problem? FCC hearing examiner James Cunningham has frequently quizzed witnesses on their own attitude toward marijuana.

Jolt to Journalism

Chi broadcast sentiment remains solidly behind WBBM-TV, with most broadcast newsmen considering the station guilty of nothing more serious than occasional lapses into naiveté. There is considerable concern that the hearings will put a damper on what little broadcast investigative journalism takes place in the Windy City.

"It's hard to generalize from this particular case," a news exec from another station said "but if we have to look over our shoulder every time we cover a controversial story, we might as well get out of investigative reporting. I can't accept the idea that a newsman must report every crime that he observes. If we must call the police before we do a story say on a gambling spot or a house of ill repute, there just won't be any story when we get there." This opinion was reflected at other stations called.

—October 16, 1968, pp. 38, 51.

TROUBLE BREWS IN CHI'S "POT"

PRIVATE HEARING SEEN OMINOUS

BY MORRY ROTH

Chicago, Oct. 22.—The last-minute appearance of a handful of CBS bigwigs failed to instill any excitement into the final days of the FCC public

hearings into WBBM-TV's Nov. '67 airing of a news special entitled "Pot Party At A University." In two hours of questioning, commission counsel Joseph Stirmer failed to elicit any substantial new information from CBS prexy Dr. Frank Stanton, and even more summary treatment was afforded CBS-owned Stations prez Robert Wood and Broadcast Group prexy John Schneider.

However desultory the public hearings, enough has leaked out from private "executive" sessions to indicate that WBBM-TV may be in hotter water than it seemed to be a week ago. In an apparent courtroom slip, FCC chief hearing examiner James Cunningham described some of the private testimony as "damaging" to the station. Questioned about it later, CBS counsel Newton Minow replied wryly: "It didn't help us."

The "Contact" in Private

The key witness affording testimony hostile to the station in the private hearings appears to be a young man referred in public either as The Contact or The Co-arranger. He is assumed to be the person whom WBBM-TV reporter John Missett contacted and who led him to the marijuana party at issue. The Contact is known to have skipped to Canada when the case came under investigation and to have returned after he was granted immunity from prosecution.

It is also understood that The Contact was "upset" at the hearings and turned against WBBM-TV. He is believed to have testified that Missett did, in fact, "arrange" the pot party, as the FCC infers. (At one point in the public hearings when Stirmer was badgering a CBS witness and Minow complained, Stirmer snapped back: "You were giving a witness of

ours a hard time only a few hours ago." It was at that time that The Contact was being interviewed in private.)

In earlier testimony, James Johnson, an N.U. graduate, testified that Missett had interviewed him two months before the show and asked him about the pot scene on campus. Johnson said that Missett had never asked him to arrange or stage a pot party. The investigation also heard testimony from a WBBM-TV marketing research exec as to the effect of the show on ratings (nil). Two psychiatrists also testified to the increasing use of pot in the middle class, and one, Dr. Jerome Jaffe, said that he saw nothing extraordinary about the show and described the whole thing as "a tempest in a teapot."

A Criminal Act?

The final day's interrogation of the CBS execs went deeply into the matter of whether Missett should have revealed the names of the pot party participants to his superiors in violation of an agreement which he had with the party guests. CBS attorney Albert Dwyer said that Missett had been asked and refused. Stirmer asked Dwyer if he had "insisted" and Dwyer said that he had not. The question is important since Illinois has no specific "press immunity" law. However, since the case has never been referred to a city, state or federal court, the question remains moot. (At one point, Dwyer revealed, CBS had Missett hire his own attorney on the basis that if Missett had actually committed a criminal act there would be a "conflict of interests" between the reporter and CBS.)

Four Month Wait

At the end of the hearings, Minow asked for and received 45 days to prepare a CBS defense summation. After that it will take the FCC another two to three months to review the material and to pass judgment. The conclusion, as one cynic noted, will come considerably after the November elections.

Aside from the testimony of The Contact or other privately-heard witnesses, the fate of WBBM-TV would seem to depend upon external circumstances. Given the current anti-video stance of the Congress and the FCC's own harrassment by the Staggers Committee and others, it is quite possible that the commission might decide to make an example of the station. An attorney indirectly connected with the case reported that fears at the station have escalated from the worry of a "wrist-slap" of two weeks ago to genuine concern that WBBM-TV might receive a temporary license or even be given such dire punishment as a license suspension.

—October 23, 1968, pp. 29, 42.

FCC EXAMINER FINDS WBBM-TV GUILTY RE "POT PARTY," RAPS CBS FOR LAPSES

Washington, Jan. 14.—CBS o&o WBBM-TV in Chicago "bungled" its responsibilities in broadcasting a "pot party" show on marijuana smoking Nov. 1 and 2, 1967, according to an initial decision released last week by FCC chief hearing examiner James D. Cunningham. The pot party "was pre-arranged for the benefit of CBS," he ruled, and never would have been held but for the request by a WBBM-TV reporter.

Cunningham made no recommendations for punishment, but simply forwarded his conclusions to the commission for its consideration. FCC action in some form is expected within a week or so.

The House Investigations Subcommittee headed by Rep. Harley Staggers (D-W.Va.) held a hearing several months ago on the tv program and the FCC's investigation of it. CBS officially, including prez Frank Stanton, then and since then have stoutly defended the show as a legitimate journalistic enterprise with social impact. The case is one that has been cited frequently in recent months as demonstrating the danger of the government looking over the newsman's shoulder.

Supervisory Lapses

The issues go far beyond the "pre-arranged" nature of the pot party. Cunningham also criticized the defensive reaction of the station and network management to charges that the show might have been rigged. The initial decision claims there were supervisory lapses at several levels. Making use of witnesses who include four whose names were not revealed because of their presence at the pot party, Cunningham concluded, in effect, that WBBM-TV reporter John V. Missett lied ("Missett's version is rejected") in telling how he and the WBBM-TV crew were invited to the pot party rather than arranging it.

After finding the pot party to have been staged for the benefit of WBBM-TV, Cunningham also concluded:

—The station's "supervisory personnel and responsible CBS officials allowed themselves, without adequate investigation, to believe what Missett, a young, ambitious reporter, told them because of their interest in the program."

—CBS "did not demonstrate adequate responsibility when it responded to the commission's initial inquiries with the general statement that it had conducted a careful and intensive investigation and concluded on the

basis thereof that the charges of staging were without foundation. It is found that this response was inadequate since the licensee failed at this time to advise the commission of its decision to respect Missett's promises of confidentiality to the participants; failed to advise the commission that these participants had not been interviewed; and failed to mention such matters as the fact that a coincidental telephone survey had been ordered for the second night of the broadcast."

—CBS's "lack of policy concerning the need to notify the authorities when it is known that a crime is about to happen, and in requiring its station managers to clear in advance proposed controversial programs, deprives the licensee of the control it must exercise over its stations in order to carry out the responsibilities to the commission."

—January 15, 1969, p. 44.

FCC SETS DATES FOR CBS ANSWER TO EXAMINER'S "POT PARTY" VERDICT; CREDIBILITY COULD BE NEW WRINKLE

BY LARRY MICHIE

Washington, Jan. 21.—CBS last week asked the FCC to schedule an oral argument on the contentions leveled by FCC Chief Hearing Examiner James Cunningham that CBS o&o WBBM-TV in Chicago flubbed its licensee responsibilities in airing a program in November 1967 about a "pot party" supposedly held on the campus of Northwestern U. in suburban

Chicago. The Commission set Feb. 17 as filing deadline for comment and said it would hear oral argument on March 3.

Delicate Questions

The case, which involved delicate judgments on journalistic latitude, is sensitive at a dozen points.

Question: Does the fact that a tv station is a Federal licensee mean that its reporters should be more hobbled than print reporters?

Should a broadcast reporter be required to inform the police if he is aware the law is about to be broken?

Should the management of a station be required to double-check controversial reports?

How literally should a licensee be held responsible for the acts of a station's management?

Does that mean that CBS, in New York, should dictate all phases of controversial programming by the Chicago management? . . .

—January 22, 1969, p. 27.

"POT PARTY" ON PAN BUT WBBM-TV LICENSE NOT "IN JEOPARDY" AS FCC HARD-RAPS KNUCKLES OF OWNER CBS

Washington, May 20.—Although the license of CBS o&o WBBM-TV in Chicago isn't "in jeopardy," the FCC last week firmly warned the station owner to set down policies to guide its personnel so there won't be a repeat of the problems that grew out of the station's two "Pot Party at a University" shows in November of 1967.

The commission chastisement might not be strong enough to please the House Investigations Subcommittee, which in the midst of the FCC investigation unveiled its own probe and indicated a belief that the outlet "staged" the programs showing the use of marijuana by students of Northwestern U. in suburban Chicago.

Relying on hearing findings by former FCC Chief Hearing Examiner James Cunningham, the commission said that it was obvious that the station knew of the pitfalls of possible staging charges, but was at fault in trusting too blindly in a young and inexperienced broadcast reporter and in not following up the commission's initial queries vigorously enough.

Commission's Summary

The FCC, relying heavily on the hands-off news policy it outlined in letters to the three networks growing out of charges of network news staging while covering the Democratic National Convention in Chicago last August, summed it up this way:

> "We are in the sensitive news field and fully recognize that we must tailor our actions to serve best the public interest in the most robust, wide-open debate—the underpinning of the First Amendment. Here there has been a serious mistake and an inadequate investigative report to the commission, which occurred because of deficient policies in the field of investigative journalism.
>
> "The license of WBBM-TV is not in jeopardy because of these mistakes. But, acting, we believe, consistently with the foregoing paramount

public interest consideration, CBS should set forth promptly and to the extent appropriate and feasible, for the guidance of its personnel, its policies in this area and, most important, to make appropriate revisions in its policies (including especially those with respect to its supervisory responsibilities) in order to make every reasonable effort to prevent recurrence of this type of mistake."

Johnson Does a Burn

Commissioner Nicholas Johnson was the only dissenter, but his views weren't ready for publication Friday (16), and his only released statement was a blast at the commission for not holding up its decision until he had his views ready for inclusion. He blamed the FCC speedup on FCC fears of news leaks in the trade press.

"We have not, therefore, in my judgment," Johnson said, "taken sufficient time to consider the serious issues involved in this case and to evolve constructive standards for what all would concede to be an extremely difficult area of law and journalism. The commission has certainly not considered this draft opinion of mine."

Commissioners Kenneth Cox and James Wadsworth both put out individual concurring statements, the former stating that his only gripe with CBS is that it wasn't more responsive to the FCC investigation and the latter complaining that the decision wasn't a little tougher with the network.

Station Cleared

The FCC absolved WBBM-TV of charges that it staged the pot party just to get a program that would hypo the ratings books. But it did say that the young reporter, John Missett, helped set up the party, that the station never checked on Missett's story but simply took his word for it, even after complaints by Northwestern U. and the FCC.

The commission said that there is no ambiguity "with respect to the most important conclusion reached, namely, that the film should not have been made because inducement of the commission of the crime involved, as the licensee recognizes, is improper and inconsistent with the public interest. We stress that our holding is limited to the fact of this case and the particular activities involved." The FCC also plainly said that, absent of inducement, "WBBM-TV could properly present a pot party as a facet of investigative journalism."

Call for Guidelines

The FCC ruled that "CBS itself has no written policies in this area of investigative journalism. As stated, the matter is left to the judgment of the station manager. We think it clearly desirable that CBS, and other licensees, set out the basic policy (e.g., whether it is permissible when a crime of violence is being permitted; etc.). While this particular station manager did not abuse his discretion in this instance, we do not believe it unreasonable that, in this difficult and sensitive area, top management should make clear the general guidelines for all its stations. Further, top management should also set the general guidelines for implementation of these policies."

—May 21, 1969, pp. 41, 52.

FCC'S JOHNSON DISSENTS STRONGLY ON "POT PARTY" AS CURBING NEWS PROBES; FEARS WEBS WILL TAKE IT LYING DOWN

Washington, May 27.—In dissenting to the FCC decision in the CBS-WBBM-TV "pot party" case, Commissioner Nicholas Johnson last week said that "the majority has established guidelines for self-censorship by the broadcasting industry in the realm of investigative news reporting—under the threat of sanctions for lack of compliance." He said that "this commission should bend over backward to encourage courageous investigative journalism—not reach out to stifle it."

The FCC ruled that a reporter at the CBS o&o in Chicago "induced" the marijuana party that served as a focal point for the station's two "pot party" shows in November of 1967, and while it said the outlet's license wasn't in jeopardy, partly because the station hadn't known all about the reporter's activities, the commission did call for stronger policies by CBS and closer supervision.

"Confronted with the question of improper conduct on the part of CBS," Johnson said, "the commission majority has responded by constructing a number of guidelines supported by miscellaneous and varying references to the term 'solicitation,' in order to warn WBBM-TV—and necessarily the rest of the

television industry as well—not to commit the 'serious mistake' of arranging (to some undefined extent) an illegal event. I believe . . . that this move is at least journalistically unwise, and may even be unconstitutional."

Vs. Case-by-Case Rulings

The youthful and controversial commissioner argued that "the integrity of the mass media is essential to its role of communicating honest opinion and accurate information. When people lose their faith in even isolated incidents of news as they are depicted to them, they will begin to distrust all news presentations. It is therefore essential that *no* element of falsity or deception creep into the news." Therefore, he said the FCC must evolve clear and broad policies, not case-by-case rulings that confuse and intimidate broadcasters.

Johnson pointed out in particular that charges of "staging" are so ambiguous that it is nearly impossible to draw clear lines.

"There seems little doubt," he said, "that deliberate violations of the majority's decision might easily lead to punitive sanctions. Indeed, one is left with the uncomfortable impression that—given the 'seriousness' of this offense—were the errant licensee someone without the political and economic power of a CBS, the sanction might well have been more than the somewhat ironic slap on the wrist administered here."

Will Webs Acquiesce?

Despite what he considers the vagueness of the FCC's decision and the threats that it poses to journalism, Johnson said: "It is my fear . . . that the broadcasting industry will find it commercially profitable simply to acquiesce in today's majority opinion. To be sure, when corporate pocketbooks have been threatened in the past, the networks have reached deep into their coffers to fight lengthy and complicated appeals all the way to the U.S. Supreme Court. That has been the case with the FCC's personal attack doctrines and its cigaret fairness ruling. The essential question now is: will they make a similar effort in this case?" If they don't, he said, "their credibility as advocates for the freedoms of speech and the press will be lost."

—May 28, 1969, pp. 45, 53.

8 Public Control

A democracy works properly only if every important democratic institution is somehow responsible and responsive to the public. The mass media are no exception to this rule. Since media executives are not elected, other means are required to insure that public opinion will play a role in the determination of media content.

Members of the public are simultaneously consumers of the mass media and potential news makers. In their role as consumers, they may want to take the media to task for supplying the wrong kind of information—too much sex or violence, not enough foreign news or hockey scores. In their role as news makers, they may want to gain access to the media to report their own views and activities--weddings and PTA meetings, strikes and demonstrations. Both the disgruntled consumer and the unheralded news maker may find to their surprise that there is little they can do to influence the content of the mass media.

Tactics for public control of the media are few and feeble. A dissatisfied newspaper reader can phone or write the editor to complain, or he can try to organize a local boycott. An angry television viewer can send in his unsolicited opinions, or he can sit and wait and hope for a rating service to solicit them some day. An individual or group with a viewpoint to present can write a letter to the editor, call up a radio talk show, or take out a paid advertisement.   These methods are better than nothing—but not much.

The access problem is by far the more serious of the two.   Dozens of special-interest groups on all sides of the political fence have come to recognize that access to the media plays a vital role in the fulfillment of their goals.   As Hazel Henderson has put it:

> The realization is now dawning on groups espousing . . . new ideas, that in a mass, technologically complex society, freedom of speech is only a technicality if it cannot be hooked up to the amplification system that only the mass media can provide.   When our founding fathers talked of freedom of speech, they did not mean the freedom to talk to oneself. .

One way to gain access to the mass media is to start your own.   The development of offset printing has fostered the growth of literally thousands of low-cost special-interest newsletters (not to mention the flourishing underground press).   Such publications are often extremely valuable, but they are in no way an adequate substitute for coverage in the local daily.

Television is a special case.   There is no real TV equivalent of the offset newsletter (though cable television may someday produce one).   To reach the viewing public, a would-be news maker must buy his own station—at a cost in the tens or even hundreds of million dollars.   The only alternative is to put political pressure on existing station owners.

Every three years a station must apply to the Federal Communications Commission for renewal of its license.   As a rule, the FCC approves the renewal automatically—but it has the power to do otherwise.   Community groups are entitled to testify at the renewal hearings, to challenge the license, and even to apply for it themselves.   They are unlikely to win.   But they are quite likely to gain substantial concessions from the beleaguered broadcaster.

The license of station KTAL-TV in Texarkana, Texas, was up for renewal in 1969.   Twelve local black groups challenged the license, charging that the station had failed to meet the needs of the black community.   Before the FCC could decide the case, an unprecedented agreement was negotiated.   A thirteen-point statement of policy was drawn up, obliging KTAL-TV to hire two black reporters, to run public service announcements from minority groups, to meet with them once a month to discuss programming plans, and so on.   In return for the station's endorsement of this statement, the black groups agreed to withdraw their license-renewal challenge.

The selection that follows includes both the statement of policy and the formal contract between KTAL-TV and the challengers.   It is a unique and formidable document.

KTAL–TV *Statement of Policy*

KTAL-TV, having in mind its duty to serve equally all segments of the public, makes the following statement of policy:

1. KTAL will continue to observe all laws and federal policies requiring equal employment practices and will take affirmative action to recruit and train a staff which is broadly representative of all groups in the community. As part of this policy, KTAL will employ a minimum of two full-time Negro reporters, one for Texarkana and one for Shreveport. These reporters will appear locally on camera. In addition, KTAL will designate one person on its program staff to be responsible for developing local public affairs programs of the type described later in this statement, and for obtaining syndicated or other programs to serve similar needs.

2. KTAL will continue to maintain and will publicize a toll-free telephone line from Texarkana to its studios in Shreveport. A person will be available in Shreveport to receive requests for news coverage and inquiries about public service announcements. KTAL will give adequate coverage to events in the state capitals of Texas and Arkansas, as well as in those of Louisiana and Oklahoma.

3. KTAL recognizes its continuing obligation to maintain appropriate facilities in Texarkana, its city of assignment. To this end, it will assign to the main studios in Texarkana a color TV camera.

This material appears in The Alfred I. DuPont–Columbia University Survey of Broadcast Journalism 1968–1969, edited by Marvin Barrett. Published by Grosset & Dunlap, Inc.

4. KTAL recognizes its obligation to present regular programs for the discussion of controversial issues, including, of course, both black and white participants. The station will not avoid issues that may be controversial or divisive, but will encourage the airing of all sides of these issues.

5. Poverty is a primary problem in KTAL's service area. KTAL is obligated to try to help solve this problem by publicizing the rights of poor persons to obtain services and the methods by which they may do so. KTAL will also inform public opinion about the problem of poverty and the steps that are being taken to alleviate it. An aggregate of at least one-half hour of programming will be devoted to this subject each month.

6. KTAL's religious programming should cover the entire range of religious thought. As part of its continuing effort to meet this obligation, KTAL will carry the religious programs offered by NBC representing the three principal American faiths. A discussion program will also be presented to explore current religious issues at least monthly. KTAL will regularly present ministers of all races on local religious programs. These ministers will be regularly rotated in an effort to represent fairly all religious groups.

7. Network programs of particular interest to any substantial group in the service area will not be preempted without appropriate advance consultation with representatives of that group.

8. KTAL is obligated to discuss programming regularly with all segments of the public. In particular, a station employee with authority to act will meet once a month with a committee designated by the parties to the petition to deny KTAL-TV's application for license renewal. Similar efforts will be made to consult other groups representing other segments of the public.

9. KTAL will regularly announce on the air that all stations must consult with all substantial groups in the community regarding community tastes and needs, and will seek suggestions on how best to render this service. These announcements will be broadcast once a week, on a weekday, between 7:00 P.M. and 11:00 P.M.

10. KTAL reaffirms its existing policy to make no unessential reference to the race of a person. In cases where such references are made, the same practice is being and will be followed for blacks as for whites. KTAL will continue to use courtesy titles for all women without regard for race.

11. KTAL will endeavor to develop and present at least monthly in prime time a regular local magazine-type program, including not only discussion but also local talent, and seeking participation from the entire service area.

12. KTAL will solicit public service announcements from local groups and organizations. Sound on film will be used more extensively in covering local news. In covering demonstrations, picketing, and similar events, KTAL-TV will seek to present the diverse views which gave rise to the event.

13. KTAL-TV's understandings are subject to all valid laws, rules and regulations of the Federal Communications Commission, and to KTAL's primary obligation as a broadcast licensee to exercise its own good faith and judgment properly to serve all members of the viewing public. It is recognized that needs and circumstances change and that events may compel departure from these undertakings. However, KTAL-TV will not depart from these undertakings without advance consultation with the affected groups in the service area and immediate notice to the Federal Communications Commission stating the reasons for the departure. In such instances KTAL will seek to adhere to the objectives of this statement by alternative action.

Agreement

KCMC, Inc., licensee of KTAL-TV, and all parties to the Petition to Deny and to the Reply filed with respect to KCMC, Inc.'s application for renewal of its television broadcast license, being hereinafter collectively referred to as "Petitioners," agree as follows:

1. KCMC, Inc., will broadcast on prime time the statement of policy attached hereto. This agreement and this statement will also be filed with the Federal Communications Commissioner as an amendment to the pending renewal application. Any material variance from said statement shall be deemed to be a failure to operate substantially as set forth in the license.

2. Simultaneously with the filing of said statement, Petitioners will join and hereby join in requesting the Federal Communications Commission to give no further consideration to the pleadings filed by Petitioners, or any of them, with respect to KTAL-TV. Petitioners also join in requesting the Federal Communications Commission to renew KTAL-TV's television broadcast license for a full term.

3. This agreement and the attached statement contain the complete agreement of the parties, and there are no other promises or undertakings, express or implied.

Signed this 8th day of June, 1969.
KCMC, Inc.—W. E. Hussman, President

Texarkana Organization—Robert D. Smith, President
Citizens Committee to Improve Local Television Service—David E. Stephens, Chairman
Carver Terrace Community Club—Eldridge Robertson, Chairman
Negro Community Leaders Committee—G. W. Thompson, M.D.
National Association for the Advancement of Colored People—Mrs. Jennie Dansby, Secretary
Texarkana Improvement Club—H. F. Langford, Jr., President
Marshall Alumni Chapter Kappa Alpha Psi Fraternity—Denzer Burke
Gamma Kappa Zeta Chapter, Zeta Phi Beta Sorority—Helen McNeal, President
Phi Beta Sigma Fraternity—M. D. Dodd, President
New Hope Baptist Church, Kiblah, Arkansas—N. E. Jones, Pastor
Lonoke Baptist Church—C. K. Yarber, Pastor
Model Cities Planning Area P7—Miss Helen S. King
Earle K. Moore, Attorney for Petitioners
James E. Greeley, Attorney for KCMC, Inc.

PART THREE
MEDIA

9 The Medium and the Message

If you were an advertiser with a product to sell, your choice of a medium for your ads would not be an arbitrary one. You would note with interest that television is by far the most emotionally involving of the mass media, offering the incredible persuasive potential of both sound and moving pictures. You would consider carefully the advantages of radio, a "background" medium that is absorbed without much attention and hence without much criticism. You would weigh these facts against the ability of newspapers to convey detailed information that the reader can study, clip and save. You would judge also the merits and demerits of magazines, billboards, direct mail promotions, and so forth. Finally, you would make the crucial decision of where to spend your advertising dollar.

The point is this: The mass media are inherently different. Some are fast, others slow. Some are shallow, others deep; some narrow, others broad. Some media are primarily for information, others for entertainment. Some appeal to the intellect, others to the emotions. Some are national and ubiquitous, others are specialized or purely local. Some are permanent and expensive, others are ephemeral and cheap. All these differences are important in understanding the potential of each medium, and the extent to which that potential is realized.

Although the differences among the media have been studied for many years, Marshall McLuhan was the first to suggest that those differences were responsible for Western civilization. According to McLuhan, the invention of the printing press spelled the end of close-knit tribal communities. The printed word, he says, requires little from the reader in the way of participation or involvement. As a result, print-oriented people have linear minds. They are orderly, logical, and individualistic.

Television, on the other hand, is for McLuhan a very ambiguous medium, requiring tremendous participation on the part of the viewer. In this, television is like interpersonal communication—it demands emotional involvement. Television-oriented people have global minds. They are emotional and tribal.

Few of McLuhan's insights have been proved, and many are unprovable. But they serve to drive home a crucial point. Different media are inherently dissimilar, in ways that have far-reaching effects on individual psychology and social structure. These differences are unaffected by the ways the media are used, by the messages they contain. As McLuhan puts it: The medium **is** the message.

The people who program the mass media have no control over the inherent characteristics of the media. They also have no control over what the audience does with their programs. Audiences use the media for their own purposes, which need not be the media's purposes. A classic study of radio soap operas, for example, found that many listeners were more interested in guidance than in entertainment. One faithful follower commented: "If you listen to these programs and something turns up in your own life, you would know what to do about it."

During a New York newspaper strike in 1945, Dr. Bernard Berelson of Columbia University interviewed sixty readers about the effects of the strike on them personally. His report ("What Missing the Newspaper Means") concluded that people read newspapers for reasons that have little to do with the news.

Another New York strike in 1958 permitted a second test of Berelson's conclusions. The selection that follows reports the results.

PENN KIMBALL

People Without Papers

IN DECEMBER 1958 a labor dispute involving members of the Newspaper
and Mail Deliverers Union caused all seven major New York City daily
newspapers to suspend publication for nineteen days. During this
period newspaper readers went without papers that normally sell more
than 5 million copies on weekdays and more than 7 million on Sundays. . . .
    In a similar situation in 1945, Dr. Bernard Berelson of Columbia's
Bureau of Applied Social Research undertook an intensive study of sixty
newspaper readers on the island of Manhattan. Berelson's study—"What
Missing the Newspaper Means"—concluded, "Thus, although almost all
the respondents speak highly of the newspaper's value as a channel of
'serious' information, only about a third of them seemed to miss it for
that purpose."
    The major part of Berelson's findings elaborated on six basic "non-
rational" gratifications supplied by reading newspapers: (1) respite and
escape from personal cares; (2) a means of achieving social prestige
when making conversation with others; (3) indirect contact with life and
moral codes in the world outside; (4) reassurance to counter the inse-
curities of modern society; (5) pleasure derived from reading itself, apart
from the content; (6) the satisfaction of "a ceremonial or ritualistic or

    From *Public Opinion Quarterly*, 23, no. 3 (Fall, 1959), 389–98. Reprinted by
permission.

near-compulsive" habit which the act of newspaper reading has become. Berelson described his results "not as scientific proof, but rather as a set of useful hypotheses." However, during the thirteen years intervening between the two newspaper strikes in the nation's largest metropolis there had been no opportunity to replicate his data. Therefore, a resurvey was launched on the eighth day of the 1958 stoppage under the direction of the author, using a corps of twenty students in the Columbia Graduate School of Journalism to augment his own interviewing.

The base of the sample used by Berelson was broadened to include all five boroughs of New York City plus Long Island and Connecticut suburbs. Interviewing areas were selected to reflect the ethnic and economic characteristics of the metropolitan area. Detailed interviews were accomplished with a total of 164 persons who affirmed that they "ordinarily read a New York City daily newspaper regularly."

Intensity of Reactions

1. *Although a variety of alternative communication channels was available to newspaperless New Yorkers, the persons interviewed in this survey were highly conscious that they were being deprived of a valued part of their daily lives. Nearly 9 out of 10 said they missed their papers. Two out of three regular newspaper readers showed intensity about their dependence upon newspapers.*

The questionnaires taken to the field were stripped of any leading references to news events taking place during the strike or mention of any specific aspects of newspaper reading. As far as possible those interviewed were encouraged to find their own words to tell how they were reacting to life without newspapers. People did react with varying degrees of intensity:

"I'm utterly lost."
"It's been just awful."
"I might as well be in Alaska, I feel so cut off."
"Being without papers is like being without shoes."

"I like to know what's going on. I listen to the radio to replace part of it. But I miss the news in the paper."

"It's damn annoying. I'm running out of magazines to read on the train."

"It's been a nuisance. I found myself phoning a radio station to get the hockey scores."

"I've become accustomed to it now. I can get along quite well without them. I do miss them a little I guess. Once they say it on the radio, it's gone forever."

"To tell the truth, I don't mind at all. It's the first time I've been able to leave the compulsion to see what's on everybody's mind. I'm getting a lot of work done. No more excuses not to get down to work." . . .

Shift to Radio News

2. *An increase in attention and time devoted to radio news broadcasts was the most striking change in media habits during the newspaper stoppage. Radio listening and TV viewing both increased. But radio newscasts attracted more new listeners and were heard with far more frequency. Although many said their appreciation of radio and TV as an "emergency" source of news had increased, there was substantial criticism of these media as substitutes for newspapers.* . . .

The "hole in the day" left by the disappearance of papers resulted in a shift toward both TV and radio, but, as the table indicates, the gains for radio were more pronounced. Cursory listening to radio fell off sharply, while those spending more than three hours at their sets showed double the increase for TV. Asked directly, 52 per cent said they were aware of listening to radio more during the newspaper stoppage, as against 35 per cent who reported watching more TV. . . .

Time Spent on Radio and Television Before and During the Strike
(*in per cent*)

	Radio Before	Radio During	Television Before	Television During
None	4	5	5	6
1–14 minutes	23	8	5	4
15–29 minutes	15	10	1	1
30 minutes–1 hour	13	10	9	9
1–2 hours	11	16	13	11
2–3 hours	12	14	25	19
Over 3 hours	22	37	42	50

Surveillance Gratifications

3. *The dominant reason volunteered for missing the newspapers was the feeling of being "out of touch" with "important happenings." Individuals spoke in broad terms—"front-page stories," "world events," "the latest news"—rather than in categories familiar to editors, such as foreign, Washington, or local news. Asked to name a specific news story which might have received major attention if the papers had come out that day, a majority could name nothing except the newspaper strike itself. The broad urge to feel "up-to-date" appeared to be an end in itself apart from the specific content of the news. Newspapers were regarded as unique in their ability to supply this satisfaction.*

Despite increased listening to radio and television and despite the fact that 50 per cent of those interviewed said they were reading more magazines and books, most expressed dissatisfaction with the available substitutes for newspapers. Six out of ten (59 per cent) mentioned very broad definitions of "news" when asked what part of the paper they missed most. The same proportion said "yes" when asked: "Are there any particular things going on now you wish you knew more about?" But, under probing, only a small minority could focus on any specific event. Their answers again tended toward generalities. When asked, "If a newspaper came out today, what do you think would be the two or three biggest stories?" most respondents drew a blank. Only one story (a crisis in Berlin over Russian demands that Western forces be withdrawn) was cited by more than 10 per cent.

Nevertheless, the disposition to say that they felt "out of touch" and that nothing was "the same as the paper" prevailed. Some need related to news was not being fulfilled by the drenching quantity of alternate media of communication. People seemed to feel drawn to the news as it appears in a newspaper without fully understanding what they get out of it, or without knowing how to analyze for themselves what it means to them. . . .

The surveillance of developments that readers have no means to anticipate but that may have an important impact on their daily lives is a well-recognized communication function. Newspapers are wide-ranging enough, apparently, for people to feel that they are monitoring nearly everything of importance. The scanning and selection process that individual readers can apply to the newspaper format seems to be satisfying in itself. Sometimes this satisfaction may involve merely finding out that nothing in the paper that day registers as being important to him. Yet he feels "up-to-date" and "informed" even though his store of positive information has not been increased. . . .

Confirmation of Berelson's Data

4. *The "nonrational" gratifications of newspaper reading enumerated by Berelson in his experimental study of a previous New York newspaper strike were confirmed by these interviews. In addition, the testimony of those interviewed suggests at least two other functions: stimulation and occupation. Boredom, as well as idleness, was evident among news-paperless residents of the New York area.*

Ample evidence was present in the reactions of the newspaper public to being without newspapers to confirm the half dozen "basic gratifications" turned up by Berelson in his earlier survey. Some examples:

1. *Respite*
   "I just can't seem to relax. I used to come home from work and re-lax with a paper. I can't relax any more. It's terrible."
   "I don't enjoy my second cup of coffee in the morning any more. With the papers, it was like a breather. Now I just stare out the window."

2. *Social prestige*
   "I'm a total loss now when somebody speaks to me about some-thing that's happening. I like to be able to keep up my end of the conversation."
   "I'm not *au courant* always now. I notice it out to lunch with my friends. The radio is no substitute for a newspaper. I like to be able to make intelligent conversation."

3. *Social contact*
   "I miss the gossip, the dirt. It's like taking part of my life away."
   "You talk about the news with your friends. I miss the Voice of the People and the Inquiring Fotographer in the *News* the most. I like to see what people have to say."

4. *Security*
   "It's pretty lonesome without papers. I feel a great void."
   "I just don't feel right, that's all. I can't put my finger on it, but it upsets me."

5. *Reading for its own sake*
   "I brought home old copies of *Newsday* from a friend's house in Nassau, just to have the papers. Television and radio have the news well covered, but it's not the same."
   "I'm retired and I usually read the papers all morning. I've had to undo all that. I'm not used to not having papers to read."

6. *Ritual*
   "In the evening I usually look forward to the papers after the dishes are done and my child is in bed. It's a habit, I guess."
   "I sleep on the sofa to make the time go before work. I work nights. Usually I lay down and read the paper. Now I just sleep."

Although Berelson mentions the function of a newspaper in trans-porting the reader outside his immediate world in connection with "res-pite" and "social contact," the longing for news of crime and human disaster expressed by some would seem to warrant a category of its own. Many had no qualms about admitting their taste for such stories. And even when articulating disapproval of these themes, others confessed to a compulsion to read them when they were available.

7. *Stimulation*

"I wish I knew more about the fires, the tragic things. Not that I like it, mind you. But I say to myself, 'There but for the Grace of God go I.'"

"I miss the murders, robberies, and killings. I've been reading the good stories in old copies of the *Daily News* all over again."

"I'm glad the papers are gone. I suddenly realized I wasn't reading a lot of gore that depressed me."

The "void," "emptiness," and "lost" feelings expressed by many respondents in this survey tell something about the nature of present-day living, as well as the meaning of newspapers. The time vacuum created by the lack of newspapers to read was only partially occupied by radio and TV. Housewives reported that they had spent some of the extra time on housework or Christmas preparations. Although a large share of those interviewed said they were reading more magazines and books during the strike, only a small percentage had actually done so during the twenty-four hours preceding the interview. A note of procrastination and guilt crept into some of these reports.

8. *Occupation*

"I'm reading Dr. Zhivago now. I've been meaning to for a long time. It would sit there on the living room table, but by the time I finished with the papers I didn't feel like starting a book."

"I made myself a suit last Sunday for the first time in my life."

"I finally got around to fixing up a few things around the house that have been piling up for a long time."

There was some increase in visiting and entertaining, especially on Sunday, and a good deal of extra sleeping. Fully a third of those interviewed were unable to say where the time had gone or conceded that they had merely idled it away.

"I just moped around."

"I guess I just sat around feeling sore because there weren't any Sunday papers."

"Everybody sits in the subway like a dope."

"I went out in the car last weekend and drove around. Stopped for a few drinks with a friend. Didn't know what to do with myself."

"I slept late instead of crawling out of bed to read the *Times*."

The sleeping, idling, and purposeless passing of time which took place during the newspaper strike were not generally enjoyed. But without newspapers many seemed to possess limited resources for occupying themselves through other means.

Differences Between Male and Female Readers

5. *Although men and women missed the papers with similar intensity and both sexes said they missed the general news most, there were differences. Advertising and the gossip columns were greatly missed by women, and nearly half of them said they altered their shopping habits during the strike. Men missed the sports pages most after the broad news categories. Education increased women's dependence upon newspapers, and college-educated women valued the papers most of all.*

Men were the dominant newspaper buyers in this sample of readers in the New York area, where home delivery is the exception. Slightly more men (65 per cent) than women (54 per cent) mentioned "headline news," "world news," "front-page news," or some variation as the part of the paper they missed most. More men than women answered in the affirmative when asked: "Are there any particular things going on now you wish you knew more about?" . . .

Women, however, were generally more articulate than men in expressing their feelings in the area described by Berelson as "nonrational gratifications." . . .

Conclusion

Large-circulation New York newspapers have less "community" flavor than the dailies in most American cities. Local news in New York encompasses a vast scene, remote from most newspaper readers' personal experience. Except for newspapers, the tremendous communications apparatus of the metropolitan area continued to function during the strike. Thus it is remarkable that metropolitan New Yorkers missed the papers as much as they did.

The gratifications discussed by Berelson and confirmed in this survey were particularly associated with newspapers by those who were interviewed. News as it is presented in newspapers had an appeal distinct from news transmitted by other media. More intensive study is required to measure the impact of printed news as distinct from other news and other forms of reading matter. This is an inviting area for further research on the meaning of newspapers to their readers.

10 Newspapers

A newspaper is an unbound, printed publication, issued at regular intervals, which presents information in words, often supplemented with pictures.

Don't memorize that definition. It is accurate, but not very useful. The following are more enlightening:

- For readers, a newspaper is a source of entertainment, service, and to a lesser extent news.
- For reporters, a newspaper is an employer, and newspapering is a difficult, relatively low-paid job in which one tries to change the world but winds up merely observing it.
- For scholars, a newspaper is a vital way to inform the public, and hence an essential ingredient of democracy.
- For publishers, a newspaper is a business.

Not surprisingly, these definitions often come into conflict.

When they do, readers and publishers have a lot more to say about the outcome than reporters and scholars. Why, for example, is 60 percent of the average daily paper made up of ads? Reporters would rather see more news, and so would scholars. But publishers prefer to print ads. And readers, as often as not, prefer to read ads. Similarly, newspaper editorials are on the decline because publishers don't like to write them and readers don't like to read them. And newspaper monopoly is on the rise because publishers earn more money that way and readers couldn't care less.

Consider another example—the syndicated feature. Syndicated comic strips, advice columns, and the like make up as much as one-third the editorial content of the average daily paper. Why? Because they are cheap; a cost-conscious publisher can use the syndicates to fill 35 percent of his news hole for only 10 percent of his editorial budget. And because they are entertaining, which is what the public wants.

Publishers and readers win most of the battles, but not all. Some improvements in newspaper journalism have taken place despite their opposition or indifference. Specialized reporting and interpretive writing are two very important examples. The need for both developments was obvious by the late 1930s. News was too complicated for reporters to understand it without specialized training or to explain it without interpretation. Yet even today most publishers and readers show little enthusiasm for these trends.

The typical reporter spends most of his time out covering stories. He works under tremendous deadline pressure, trying to get the news as quickly and accurately as he can. Unlike broadcast newsmen, he must provide details, background, and interpretation—not just the headlines. Unlike magazine newsmen, he must do the job in minutes—not days. And if the story is complex and specialized, his task is that much harder.

The selection that follows chronicles a day in the life of Dana Bullen, Supreme Court reporter for the Washington **Evening Star.** Bullen's beat is one of the most challenging in the nation, and one of the most important. As you read the selection, keep two facts in mind: (1) The **Star's** publisher probably cares very little about the quality of his paper's Supreme Court coverage. (2) The average **Star** reader cares even less.

DAVID L. GREY

Decision-Making by a Reporter
Under Deadline Pressure

Throughout the October–June term of the Court, Bullen has become familiar with the 100–150 detailed cases that the Court will rule on during the term. But he has no idea what specific decisions will be handed down on any specific opinion day. By this day, May 24, there are about 15 cases with written opinions left to be announced plus possible numerous Court orders granting or denying review of lower court decisions. With a couple of decision days likely still left in the term, the Justices may announce anywhere from one to two to perhaps more than half a dozen decisions.

Bullen faces three deadlines for the *Star's* main editions—(at the time) 10:55 a.m. (main area edition), 12:15 p.m. (primarily home delivery) and 1:25 p.m. (primarily street sales).

The Justices will convene at 10 a.m. sharp in the Courtroom on the main (first) floor of the Court building.

Bullen enters the Court building about 9:15 a.m. and goes directly to the cafeteria in the basement for breakfast.

9:38 a.m.—Bullen enters his basement office. He has just found out from the Court Press Officer that there are 175 lawyers to be sworn in, which will take easily a half hour. He sees red light attached to phone that means office has called while he was away.

From *Journalism Quarterly,* 43, no. 3 (Autumn, 1966), 419–28. Reprinted by permission. Dr. Grey's discussion of his method and findings has been omitted from this excerpt.

9:40—Calls office. No one has yet been assigned to cover special ceremony for former Justice Burton, who recently died. Former President Truman is not coming, which takes some of the edge off the occasion. Asks how manpower situation is and lets it be known that he has a busy day. Situation left that someone else will cover the ceremony.

9:42—Calls national news desk and tells editor that there are 175 lawyers being admitted to practice, including a Catholic nun. Says he assumes one of the wire services is following up on the nun. Matters left that way.

9:45—Takes off suit coat and sits back in swivel chair. Starts reading the morning Washington *Post*. Flips and scans pages.

9:47—Sees article on (then) Justice Goldberg speaking at a Unitarian Church. Tears article from paper.

9:50—Throws *Post* into nearby wastebasket and starts skimming the New York *Times*. Wants to make sure nothing has happened that might affect a Court story—such as Billie Sol Estes out on bail.

9:51—Tears out Fred Graham story from San Juan, Puerto Rico, on Bar meeting and tosses onto desk with other article.

9:52—Tears out small "personal item" and stuffs in shirt pocket.

9:53—Rips out story on false arrests in New York. Might be worth checking locally sometime. Tears out article on anti-trust actions in bank mergers.

9:54—Throws *Times* into wastebasket.

9:55—Several newsmen from wire service (with whom he shares office) enter room—one is a photographer who wants to get picture of the nun with her sponsor, Senator Hart from Michigan. The five-minute warning buzzer sounds.

9:56—Leaves office with pencils for sharpening and to see if he can "find out any clues."

9:57—Returns with sharpened pencils. Press Officer still out getting the stack of written opinions.

9:58—Leaves for washroom. Wire service men leave. Room now empty.

10:02—Press Officer wheels opinions down hall on cart to Press Room near Bullen's office. Bullen re-enters office. Has been told by Press Officer there may be "one good one." Starts thinking in terms of Billie Sol Estes case (on television in Texas courtroom) or birth control case (on ban of birth control clinic in Connecticut).

10:03—Decides not to call office yet. Pulls out folders and starts sorting through file on Estes. Folder consists of 20–25 sheets of paper with clippings attached, plus typed and penciled notes. Several paragraphs of background material are marked boldly alongside clippings of earlier story. These could be used again—"lifted out" nearly verbatim, if necessary. Starts to skim pages, looking for the main ideas, occasionally marking sections with large crosses or stars.

10:07—Starts to look at birth control story folder. This consists of 15–20 pages. Makes special note with red pencil that law is 86 years old. Comes across background memorandum of case prepared by the Association of American Law Schools. Memo is heavily underlined and is skipped over. "Too late if don't know now."

10:10—Turns to folder on anti-trust cases. Bullen's reaction: these are complicated.

10:12—Continues skimming the 4–5 pages, again marking stars with red pencil next to passages.

10:15—Looks at a labor case.

10:16—Looks at a case on Communists in labor union offices.

10:17—Looks at case involving destroying of Communist mail by the Post Office. Briefs had been read earlier; skimming used here as a "refresher process."

10:18—A *Star* business page reporter enters room, says hello, heads for couch and sits down with a copy of the *Times*. Bullen comments that there may be only three or four opinions and that it's uncertain if there will be any stories for business page reporter to handle. Reporter nods and continues reading.

10:19—Bullen gets up and walks to cabinet to check wire service file of briefs on Communist mail case. (There are three full sets of briefs—one for both the Associated Press and United Press International and one for all the other Court newsmen. The file is handy and is used fairly often—with permission.) Checks name of propaganda publication involved.

10:20—Returns to desk.

10:23—Looks at folder on natural gas rate cases.

10:24—Goes out of room "to see what's happening."

10:25—Returns to office, sits down and leans back in chair.

10:27—Gives copy of resolution honoring Justice Burton to business page reporter—pointing out that it is self-explanatory.

10:28—Looks up at wall clock and notes that the 10:55 deadline nears. Looks out window and continues to lean back in chair.

10:31—Gets up suddenly and goes out of office. The business page reporter continues to read the resolution honoring Justice Burton.

10:33—Bullen returns, hands file on Justice Burton to business page reporter. Says photographer will be in for the 11 a.m. ceremony. Does other reporter want to stay around? Yes. It's agreed.

10:38—Both continue to flip through clip files and folders.

10:45—Other reporter leaves room.

10:46—A rattling in the air tubes from the Courtroom to the Press Room can be heard. (This is the sign that the first opinion is on its way —a tube containing a slip of paper with the case number on it is being sent to the Press Officer who will then release decision to the news media.)

10:47—*Star* copy boy enters office with copy of majority opinion. It's case #291—an anti-trust case in three parts. Bullen checks the vote. It's 5–2, with two Justices not participating. Checks personal file. Finds one paragraph. Case appears to be relatively minor anti-trust issue. Question: should he try to handle case in a couple of paragraphs at end of his story or should he let the business reporter handle it.

10:49—Calls national desk. Flips pages while resting phone receiver on his shoulder. Tells desk that first opinion out and that "it's a small business" thing. Holds off any decision until sees what else is coming that day.

10:50—Notes that first opinion was by Justice Clark—thus only the senior-most Justices left for the day. (Justices announce opinions in order of seniority—those shorter in time on Court come first.) Continues to glance through the opinion.

10:53—Copy boy enters again. Press Officer says this is the "best thing" for the day. It's the Communist mail case, *Corliss Lamont* v. *Postmaster General.*[1]

10:54—The Court has struck down the Post Office practice of withholding propaganda mail and destroying it unless requested by the addressee to be delivered. Vote is 8–0 in two parts. Bullen circles name of the majority opinion writer and writes in the vote on the first page. He starts to read the majority opinion, underlining quickly as he goes.

(10:55—First deadline passes.)

10:57—Copy boy comes in with the next case—#421—a Federal Communications Commission decision involving use of confidential documents. "It's not big." After glancing to see what it is Bullen puts it on top of railing alongside his desk.

10:58—Continues to read the Communist mail case. Continues to mark passages of majority opinion.

11:00—Copy boy brings in another case. It's a right-to-legal-counsel issue in three parts. It's put aside immediately. Bullen picks up the phone and calls the national copy desk. He's ready to dictate. It's agreed business story goes to business page reporter.

11:01—As dictationist at other end of phone gets ready, Bullen lays out the opinion and folders in front of him. He gives the story the identifying slugline "Mail" and starts to dictate: "The Post Office Department practice—of holding up mail believed to be foreign propaganda . . ." Double buzzer sounds indicating end of Court action for the day.

11:02—The copy boy brings in the orders of the Court—the last items that will be handed down. Bullen continues: ". . . was struck down today by the Supreme Court as an infringement of . . .

11:03—"First Amendment rights, period, paragraph. Justice William O. Douglas, who delivered the Court's (unanimous)[2] opinion,—

11:04—". . . said the decision was based on the fact that an addressee (a-d-d-r-e-s-s-e-e) was required to request that such detained mail be delivered . . . period, paragraph. 'This requirement is almost certain to have a deterrent effect'—Douglas said . . . 'especially as respects to those that have sensitive positions' . . ."

11:05—Continues this procedure of filing story. Alternates between the opinion itself and paraphrasing of clippings and other notes.

11:24—Puts phone down briefly, pauses. Problem is minor one of wording—wants to leave situation a bit open because of possibility that change in Post Office procedure might bring different Court ruling later. Inserts phrase to this effect.

11:28—Tells dictationist at other end of phone to send copy along to national desk. Calls national desk to inform them insert is on the way.

11:30—Back to the dictationist and the story.

11:34—Looks at the concurring opinion by Justice Brennan for the first time.

11:35—Rests phone on shoulder. Reads opinion quickly.

11:37—Tells dictationist to mark another insert. Checks wall clock —12:15 deadline is nearing. "Let me call you back. OK?" Cuts off line.

11:38—Dials national desk. Tells them another insert is coming.

11:40—Back to the dictationist. Makes a high insert based on concurring opinion.

11:42—Resumes quote from concurring opinion, attributing remarks to Justice Goldberg.

11:45—Corrects mistake; Justice Goldberg had concurred in the opinion but it was written by Justice Brennan.[3]

11:46—Bullen expresses concern over the actual vote. Is opinion really unanimous? Decision is 8–0 but three Justices are part of concurring opinion that has slightly different emphasis.

11:48—Resumes main part of story, emphasizing the fact that three Justices concurred with slightly different view on the issue.

11:51—Tells dictationist to send along what he has so far.

11:52—Wonders whether sent too much—but this seems to be the only thing that is "real newsy" so decided could go a little longer than usual.

11:53—Tells dictationist to hold on. Starts to scan other opinions left. Tells dictationist: "Mark 'folo'—The Court also had these other actions—"

11:54—Starts dictating civil rights story based on a brief unsigned order. This follows the Communist mail story. After a lead paragraph, picks up four or five prepared paragraphs and reads from these. Shows first obvious sign of relaxing.

12:01—Starts dictating short story about Court agreeing to review libel case.

12:03—Scans other orders—pauses on Court refusal to hear a conviction of a home repairs firm. Checks notes and starts dictating short story.

12:11—Sets phone receiver down and looks at FCC opinion announced by Court.

12:13—Turns to notes on case.

12:15—Spots summary paragraph in opinion, picks up phone receiver and quickly dictates paragraph. (Second deadline passes.)

12:16—Turns to opinions in right-to-counsel case. It was sent back with no Court action. Seems to involve habeas corpus questions.

12:17—Looks through concurring opinion in the case and starts to file another "folo" item. Stops, reads more of opinion.

12:24—Calls national desk to tell them he has a final news story that might be interesting. It may be a "sleeper"—including several views by the Justices on procedural matters in criminal cases.

12:27—Reporter for second wire service (who has a separate office in main Press Room) enters Bullen's office. Bullen asks what reporter is doing on the right-to-counsel case. Reporter answers that he is going to read over it slowly—hasn't decided yet. Reporter asks about identification of person in civil rights case. Bullen says he isn't using the name. Reporter leaves and heads back toward Press Room; Bullen resumes study of right-to-counsel case.

12:30—Bullen asks wire service reporter across the room (with whom he shares office) whether reporter sees any "barnburners." Reply: Only the Communist mail case.[4]

12:33—Talks with national desk. It's agreed to file separate story on criminal procedures matter. Wire service reporter leaves desk and goes out of room.

12:34—Bullen starts dictating story.

12:38—Shows sign again of relaxing.

12:42—Pauses, checks clock.[5] The 1:25 deadline nears but is fairly far off.

12:47—Wire service reporter returns to desk—observes to wire service colleague that reporter (in Press Room) for competitive service is giving considerable attention to procedural matter story. Starts reading the opinion quickly.

12:48—Bullen finishes dictating. "That's all." Hangs up phone.

12:50—Starts checking through rest of orders.

12:51—Spots case not on previous order lists.

12:52—Checks case—finds it of primarily minor procedural interest. Decides not worth story.

12:53—Goes back to list. Calls national desk again.

12:54—Smiles, body relaxes.

12:55—"All I have for you." Hangs up phone.

The proceeding sequence can also be looked at schematically in an effort to get an overview of the patterns of news information in and news flow out.

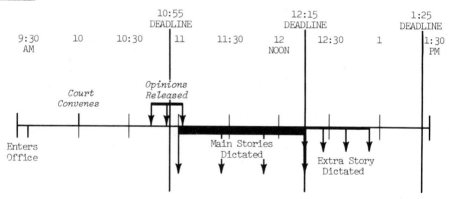

DECISION DAY AT THE COURT (MAY 24, 1965)

COURT INPUT:

NEWSMAN'S OUTPUT:

Washington Star newsman faced three deadlines—10:55 a.m., 12:15 and 1:25 p.m. Court's opinions were released within 15 minutes—10:46 to 11:01. Dictation of No. 1 story started at 11 and lasted until 11:51 with remaining stories squeezed in before main 12:15 deadline. Special story and other items were handled from 12:15 to 12:55: reporter, thus, finished 30 minutes before final deadline.

Everything but the criminal procedure story made the main 12:15 and 1:25 p.m. deadlines on May 24. (The first five paragraphs of the Communist mail story also made a replate of the 10:55 a.m. edition.) In total, all these May 24 stories ran about 1,100 words, or 34 column inches based on an 8-column format. The criminal procedure story, which ran about 450 words or another 13 column inches, appeared in all major editions of the *Star* on May 25.   In addition, among other activities on the afternoon of the 24th, Bullen put together a follow-up story for the 25th that stressed Congressional and Post Office Department reaction to the Communist mail case.

---

[1] Eventually cited as 381 U.S. 301 (1965).

[2] Exact word missed by the observer, but Bullen said afterwards he was quite sure he had said "unanimous."

[3] This mistake turned out to be one of those dilemma moments for the observer. Bullen had obviously misspoken.   Should the observer speak up or remain silent? Bullen likely would catch the error or the copy desk would soon do so.   But they might not.   To become a participant would be improper research procedure, but to hold back in this situation might later upset the whole observation relationship.   The "jump judgment" was made to step out of character and to point out the discrepancy. At the time and in retrospect, the important observation point seemed to be that the newsman's eye had caught the wrong name.   How the error would be corrected— or even if it would be—seemed secondary.

[4] The wire service reporter and several of his colleagues had returned to office 10–15 minutes earlier but exact time not recorded.

[5] Believed caused partly because observer had looked up at the wall clock.   Bullen had just swung around so that the observer suddenly was in his line of vision.

11 Magazines

Caskie Stinnett, former editor of **Holiday** magazine, tells this story, which he says "really sums up the magazine business today." Stinnett was on a travel junket to Portugal with a number of other writers, including **Holiday** contributor Marc Connelly. At a reception for the mayor of Lisbon each visitor was asked to stand and identify his magazine. Connelly announced that he represented **Popular Wading**, a journal for enthusiasts of shallow-water sports. It specialized, said Connelly, in medical articles, particularly the ravages of immersion foot.

Comments Stinnett: "It was hilarious, and we were all howling. But you know, I don't think anyone would laugh today. In fact, I'll almost bet that somewhere out there, you could find a special-audience magazine for waders."

The typical magazine of the past was a potpourri of features and fiction, aimed at a general audience. Such magazines still exist, but today they are losing money. Television killed them. Not that TV has appreciably dampened the public's appetite for general magazines. What TV did was to drain off the general magazine's principal advertisers—and thus its principal source of revenue.

Take **Life**, for instance. In 1970, a minute of time on NBC's **Laugh-In** (with 17 million viewers) sold for $3.82 per thousand households. A full-page four-color ad in **Life** (with 7 million readers) ran $7.16 per thousand households.   Not surprisingly, most advertisers preferred **Laugh-In** to **Life.**   Each copy of **Life** brings an average subscription price of twelve cents—yet it costs forty-one cents to edit, print, and distribute. For **Life** to break even, advertisers must cough up the remaining twenty-nine cents per copy.   But at the start of 1970, ad revenues amounted to only twenty-seven cents per copy.   Every week **Life** was actually losing two cents on each copy sold.

It has taken the magazine industry nearly twenty years to learn that it cannot beat television at the numbers game.   In the process, such giants as **Collier's, Coronet, Women's Home Companion, Look,** and the **Saturday Evening Post** have died (several reappeared with new publishers and new formats).   But magazines offer the advertiser something that neither television nor any other medium can provide: a specialized national audience.

Suppose you were a manufacturer of low-calorie foods.   If you could afford it, you'd probably advertise on television and in the newspapers. But despite the higher cost per thousand readers, you certainly would not miss a chance to take out an ad in **Weight Watchers Magazine.**   The average reader of that publication is far more likely to be interested in your product (and hence your ad) than the average newspaper reader or TV viewer.

Though not all of them go as far as **Weight Watchers Magazine** or **Popular Wading,** the most successful magazines today are specialized. **Playboy** is aimed at young, urban males with money to spend.   **Seventeen** appeals to teenage girls with fashion on their minds.   **Sunset** is for West Coast housewives and homeowners.   The **New Yorker** is for urbane, sophisticated Easterners.   **Newsweek** is for busy executives who need a concise review and interpretation of the week's events.   Each of these publications is profitable.   Each has its own devoted readers, and its own equally devoted advertisers.

Once upon a time, a strong-willed would-be editor started a newspaper.   Today, he is far more likely to start a magazine.   All he has to do is to find a group of readers with no magazine of their own, and a group of advertisers with no way to reach those readers.   If the need he sees is really there, and the magazine he produces really fills it, he is bound to succeed.

Helen Gurley Brown is such an editor.   She did not start **Cosmopolitan,** but since taking over in 1965 she has changed the magazine completely.   The selection that follows describes the change.

LEE NOURSE PATTERSON

For Hopeful Husband Hunters,
Helen Gurley Brown Has the Answers

A girl can do almost anything she really wants to do, don't you agree? She can tan instead of burn, look sexy but also look like a lady, have a job that pays because she's smart and still stay fascinating to men. I've done all these things, and thank goodness there's one magazine that seems to understand me—the girl who wants everything out of life. I guess you could say I'm That Cosmopolitan *Girl.*

So says a smooth and sexy career girl leaning out of one of *Cosmopolitan* magazine's promotional ads. Actually, however, the magazine is aimed at just the opposite sort of reader: a single woman, eighteen to thirty-four years old, who is neither beautiful nor self-confident and who *is* worried about finding a man.

This profitable recipe has been concocted by Helen Gurley Brown, *Cosmopolitan's* editor for the last three years. Mrs. Brown, the author of the best-selling book *Sex and the Single Girl,* has breathed vigorous life into what was a dying publication. In one of the fastest and most remarkable successes in publishing history, she has changed a humdrum women's magazine into a sort of female *Playboy.*

Message: Any Girl Can Get a Man

There is a trend today toward transferring popular ideas from one medium to another. Best-selling books become plays and movies;

From *Magazines in America—1968,* Communication Department, Stanford University, 1968, pp. 5–6. Reprinted by permission.

movies become television series.   Mrs. Brown has capitalized considerably on this trend.   Having sold *Sex and the Single Girl* to the movies for $200,000, she then set about spreading her message in magazine form.   Before coming to *Cosmopolitan,* she had never even worked for a magazine; but she relied on her remarkable rapport with America's single-girldom.   The new *Cosmopolitan* amplifies the book's thesis: with a little help, any girl can get a man.

Mrs. Brown believes that this message has a huge audience that other women's magazines ignore.   *McCall's, Ladies' Home Journal,* and *Redbook* are family-oriented; *Vogue, Harper's Bazaar,* and *Glamour* aim for the high fashion set.   "These magazines," says Mrs. Brown, "all assume their readers have men in their lives.   Well, there are 25 million women—many of them divorced or separated—who don't.   Her hypothesis has held.   Since she took over in 1965, *Cosmopolitan's* circulation has increased 16 per cent, to more than one million, and advertising revenues have more than doubled, to $3,600,000.

"A Sophisticated Older Sister"

The magazine (Mrs. Brown likes to think of it as a "sophisticated older sister") is jammed with advice about diets, exercise, yoga, hairstyling, and nose-straightening.   The reader is tipped off about a new pill ("a honey of a hormone") to make her more "responsive" and is told how to assemble a stock portfolio, play the guitar, and buy art to improve her mind.   *Cosmopolitan* offers guidance on landing a date at a cocktail party ("Carry a pencil and paper in your handbag in case the man asks you for your number and doesn't have the props with him"), telling horoscopes, analyzing *his* handwriting ("The man with muddy writing is a bad risk"), and being romantic ("It's a passionate moment. The phone rings.   Let it.").

Cosmopolitan is also a guide to happy mate-hunting grounds.   Canada, with "200,000 men" on the loose, is a "veritable game preserve of salesmen and business executives who fly in regularly from all over the world to . . . close important deals."   In England, where "the remnants of Victorianism have been bundled on the bonfire," unrestrained sex is the name of the game.

As *Cosmopolitan* sees it, there is almost no human activity into which sex cannot be introduced.   The magazine's main concern is the reader's emotional—that is, her *sexual*—needs.   The sexual drive in woman is a frequent theme with innumerable variations.   Scarcely a potential anxiety has not been fully aired on *Cosmopolitan's* pages.   Various articles tell the reader how to: be a lady while dating a married man; make a man out of her husband; avoid sexual entanglements with Daddy; make the most of "brief encounters"; get married; and get divorced.

Simple, Hedonistic Philosophy

The philosophy is simple and hedonistic: old-fashioned morality is *out* if it interferes with fun and excitement. Affairs and divorces are *in*, provided the woman can handle the consequences. As Mrs. Brown says, "It is no longer a question of whether she does or she doesn't. She does. The question is, can she cope?" To help her reader cope, Mrs. Brown speaks softly and carries a big blue pencil when she edits copy. The magazine, she says, *does* have a style: "not nonintellectual, not village idiot, not murky, and—please—not obscure."

Cosmopolitan also prints book, record, and movie reviews and short novels and stories. Mrs. Brown says such features help show that her publication is "not just a pippy-poo magazine." Nevertheless, the recurrent emphasis is on showing the reader how to be feminine. Mrs. Brown seems to be living proof of her own prescription. "I had very little going for me," she says; yet, at age thirty-seven, she managed to catch a "brainy, charming, and sexy husband." She considers it a monument to the effectiveness of her philosophy that such a flat-chested, not-very-pretty girl could be so successful. "It's just a half-baked crusading idea, I guess," she admits, "but I think I can help other women. I have something to say."

Convoluted Eighty-year History

Before Mrs. Brown took charge of *Cosmopolitan*, a Hearst publication, the management was wondering whether the magazine had any purpose or any future. At various times in its convoluted eighty-year history, it had been a news periodical (Winston Churchill was a regular contributor), a muckraking exposer of sleazy scandals, and an organ of distinguished fiction (by such authors as Ernest Hemingway and Theodore Dreiser). But by 1950 the popularity of *Cosmopolitan* and other general-interest magazines was waning. With an annual loss of $1,500,000, *Cosmopolitan* might have been the first to go—except for $2,500,000 worth of subscriptions that would have to be refunded if publication stopped. So Hearst cut the magazine's budget in half and raised subscription rates to discourage new subscribers. *Cosmopolitan* tried to sustain itself through newstand sales by printing lurid come-ons ("Four lousy husbands explain why"; "A kept woman explains her life"). To everyone's surprise, the magazine began to make money; and the Hearst Corporation, never known for chucking profitable operations, let it run.

Things went smoothly until the 1960's, when the newsstand sales of most magazines began to drop. *Cosmopolitan* had come to depend almost entirely on such sales. Meanwhile, many women's advertisers were throwing their accounts to more lavish magazines like *McCall's* and *Ladies' Home Journal*. Although *Cosmopolitan* was still earning about $500,000 a year, its editor, Robert G. Atherton, foresaw possible disaster. He tried to spruce up his magazine's shabby appearance and fill its pages with learned articles on law and medicine. But his plans would take money; and Hearst, unconvinced that intellectual content would hold a magical attraction for readers, said no. By 1964, with advertising and circulation sliding at an alarming rate, Hearst decided that Atherton would have to go. In came Helen Gurley Brown. She reorganized the layout completely, discarded archaic type faces, cut out big black headlines, and put catchy come-ons and chic women with low necklines on the cover.

Still Behind the Big Leaguers

What will Hearst do with its roaring success? Without any changes, *Cosmopolitan* is likely to continue roaring. But, to attain a big league position like that of *McCall's* or *Ladies' Home Journal*, and to put its circulation on a more stable subscription basis, the magazine will have to spend some money. So far, Hearst has not raised Mrs. Brown's editorial budget. *Cosmopolitan* still trails the big leaguers in paper quality, color reproduction, editorial staff size, and ability to pay top writers and photographers. Hearst will have to cultivate a new group of advertisers, since it probably cannot get much from the home appliance, furniture, and food advertisers that have been the staples of women's magazines.

Cosmopolitan is often charged with portraying a sex-charged world as unreal as *Playboy's* (though somewhat less affluent). As in *Playboy*, children seldom appear—they interfere with a free sex life. Some critics think that, to avoid boring its readers, *Cosmopolitan* must broaden its perspective beyond the single objective of catching a man. They note that Mrs. Brown's second book, *Sex and the Office*, sold only a third as many copies as *Sex and the Single Girl*, of which it was quite repetitious.

Mrs. Brown believes, however, that single girls *and* their problems will be around for a while—and that more and more of them will look to *Cosmopolitan*. "I'm a materialist," she says, "and it's a materialistic world. Nobody is keeping a woman from doing everything she wants to do but herself."

12 Broadcasting

Broadcasting—especially television—is by far the most powerful and ubiquitous of the mass media. Just about every American family owns a TV set, and the average set is on for roughly six hours a day. The potential (for good or for harm) of such a medium is incalculable.

What do American broadcasters do with this potential? They entertain. They program hour after hour of soap operas and situation comedies, westerns and detective thrillers, sporting events and music. The typical television station offers perhaps three hours of nonentertainment programming a day. Half of this is news—mostly headlines, sports, weather, and human-interest film clips. The other half is devoted to early-morning agricultural and religious shows, plus an occasional prime-time documentary. The remaining seventeen-odd hours of the broadcast day are filled with light entertainment.

Americans are so accustomed to this emphasis that they tend to assume it is inherent in the broadcast medium. But in the developing countries of Asia, Africa, and South America, broadcasting is used almost exclusively for education and information—usually as a government monopoly. American broadcasting is entertainment-centered because American broadcasters want it that way. They want it that way because they believe (rightly or wrongly) that that is what the public and the advertisers want.   But broadcast advertising is not inevitable either; there are many countries without it.   And it is at least possible to give the public what someone thinks it should want instead of what it does want.

It is arguable that the American system of broadcasting is the best possible system.   But it is not, at any rate, the only possible system.

The fact that American broadcasting is mostly entertainment does not lessen its effects on American society.   No doubt our country would be a different place without televised moon landings and election results, assassinations and battles.   But it would also be a different place without TV coverage of the World Series and the Academy Awards. Westerns and soap operas teach us something.   They reflect and reinforce certain characteristic national traits—competition and aggression, materialism and racism, humor and openness, faith and ambition.   It is as entertainers that the broadcast media have their greatest impact on American culture.

Broadcast entertainment has been attacked from many quarters. Some observers claim that televised pap is degrading American culture. Others argue that televised sex and violence are perverting American morals.   Nearly everyone agrees that too much of broadcasting is entertainment, and that too much of the entertainment is poor.

The quality of broadcast programming is determined by the structure of the industry.   It **is** an industry—and an immensely profitable one at that.   Its money-making potential depends on nationwide networks that produce popular programs capable of attracting huge audiences— huge enough to entice an advertiser to foot the bill.   If ten million Americans wanted to watch opera on TV, then NBC would produce it and General Foods would sponsor it.   But the potential audience for television opera is measured only in the tens of thousands.   And so there is little or no opera on television.

Broadcast programming is unlikely to change unless the structure of the broadcast industry changes first.   The federal government, which must approve the license of every broadcaster, has the power to force such a change.   But it is reluctant to do so directly.   Instead, the Federal Communications Commission has encouraged the growth of three new developments: satellite television, cable television, and educational television.

The selection that follows deals with educational TV station WMSB, owned and operated by Michigan State University.   WMSB is one of roughly 200 noncommercial television stations in the country today. Like most of the others, it accepts no advertising; it is supported entirely by donations from individuals and grants from companies, foundations, and the government.   The freedom of educational television from ad-

vertisers, and from the necessity to attract a mass audience, is supposed
to result in aggressive, intelligent, high-quality programming.   As the
selection indicates, it does not always work out that way.

MALCOLM BOYD

A Play Called Boy

Following my return in 1961 from a Freedom Ride, I wanted to make a
statement about race and humanness in the idiom of the theater.   I
wrote a one-act play entitled *Boy*. It is a two-person play, featuring a
Negro shoeshine man and a white man who brutalizes him.   The first
performance of *Boy* took place in a Detroit coffeehouse theater in the
spring of 1962.

When, in the fall of 1963, WMSB, the educational television station
at Michigan State University, asked if it might produce the play, I gave
my consent.   I had no idea then that the matter would end in a violent
and confused controversy, or that it would be described as an incident
raising "the issues of obscenity and profanity for both society and the
Church" (according to William Stringfellow, writing in *Motive* for May,
1965).

Boy has been performed in every section of the country by university,
civil rights and religious groups.   In southern California it was presented
widely by the Kairos Theatre Group.   It was presented in 1964 on a
tour of eastern university campuses and, at the Massachusetts Institute
of Technology, was staged in the chapel directly in front of the altar.   In
April, 1965 *Boy* was done inside the National Cathedral in Washington,
D.C. before some 5,000 persons.   NBC-TV televised an excerpt from it,
at the same time, on the *Sunday* show.   In July of the same year the play
was presented in Negro churches throughout rural Mississippi, Alabama
and Arkansas.   In August, 1964 *Boy* was seen by 12,000 youths attending

Reprinted by permission from *Television Quarterly*, the Journal of the National
Academy of Television Arts and Sciences, 4, no. 4 (Fall, 1965), 25–32.   A response
to this article by WMSB station manager Armand L. Hunter ("The Case of the
Missing *Boy*") may be found in *Television Quarterly*, 4, no. 4 (Fall, 1965), 33–39.

the Luther League Convention of the American Lutheran Church in Detroit and, in August, 1965, by nearly 10,000 youths attending the Lutheran Church in America Youth Conference in Miami Beach, Florida. Most university campuses have seen the play.

This is the same play banned by WMSB because "it contains too many curse words" and later attacked by a bishop (who had not read or seen it, but was reacting to newspaper accounts of the ETV station's censorship of it) for allegedly employing "vulgarity and profanity."

Let me relate the events leading to censorship of *Boy* by WMSB. During the summer of 1963, Robert Sherwood, then a producer-director at WMSB, expressed an interest in presenting three of my plays, including *Boy*, on the station. The other two were *Study in Color* and *The Job. . . .*

Several months passed before I next heard from Robert Sherwood, following his initial expression of interest in my writing. "I have read the plays of *Study in Color* and I am anxious to try putting them on television," he wrote me November 5, 1963. . . .

Soon afterward he came to Detroit to outline his plans, and we agreed on them. Mr. Sherwood proceeded with production arrangements. In January, 1964 Woodie King, Jr. and Cliff Frazier (actors who had appeared in the initial performances of my plays) went to East Lansing from Detroit to tape *Boy* and *The Job* for WMSB. A week later Mr. King and I were in East Lansing to tape *Study in Color* in the WMSB studios.

As Mr. Sherwood had expressed considerable satisfaction with the tapes, I was jolted when, on March 9, I received a letter from him which stated: "I am very sorry and embarrassed to have to inform you that we cannot broadcast *Study in Color, Boy* and *The Job*. The Director of Broadcasting Services made the final decision on the point that the plays do not reflect the proper function of the University in either approach or method of dealing with the social questions involved."

He added: "Please accept my apology for the problems and inconvenience I have caused and for any embarrassment I may have inadvertently caused you. In spite of the negative outcome, I still do not regret making the tapes. In fact, given opportunity, I would probably try the whole thing again and for the same reason—I still believe they ought to be broadcast."

Upon receipt of this letter, I asked Mr. Sherwood to come to Detroit for another meeting with me. I informed him that the cancellation was unacceptable to me and asked for clarification. His reply was that there was great controversy within the station management concerning the plays, with one executive claiming they were "anti-white." . . .

Incidentally, Mr. Sherwood did not mention that WMSB took exception to any objectionable words or language in the plays. This was soon to become a major issue.

Mr. Sherwood then entered into further discussions with the station. I was informed that *The Job* and *Study in Color* would be scheduled for viewing on WMSB, but *Boy* would be censored. . . .

The telecast of *The Job* and *Study in Color* was scheduled for July 12, 1964 on WMSB. I telephoned Mr. Sherwood four days before that date to ask again if *Boy* would definitely not be shown. He said it would not because it was considered "too strong" by some executives at the station. On July 11, one day before the telecast, I announced to the press that *Boy* was being censored by WMSB.

On July 12 the Sunday edition of the Detroit *News* front-paged the headline: "MSU BANS CHAPLAIN'S PLAY ON TV." "He certainly has been censored," Armand Hunter, director of the division of broadcasting at MSU, was quoted as saying. The reason given was "because officials at the East Lansing school say it 'contains too many curse words.'" (The so-called curse words were two: "damn" and "nigger," the latter being used, of course, as an exhibit in the anatomy of racial prejudice.)

Robert Sherwood was quoted by the *News:* "The play *Boy* is the best thing we have had on the station yet. It's the kind of thing that needs to be seen because of its strong message and dramatic presentation." Armand Hunter was further quoted: "I don't see the need for all the cursing. Mr. Boyd has been censored largely because television is not the place for the dialogue contained in his play."

I told the *News:* "I think the play was just too strong for the university people to take because I feel it cuts deeply and gets to the heart of what race discrimination is all about." . . .

Mr. Hunter clarified his position in his remarks to the *Free Press:* "We would have screened the play if the words had been left out," he said. According to the paper, he explained how "the two words have never been used over the station in his eight years as director" and that "they were not vital to Boyd's play." (Commenting on the incident a few days later, the Ann Arbor *Michigan Daily* quoted Mr. Hunter's remark that the words "damn" and "nigger" had never been used over the station in his eight years, and went on to say how this "speaks volumes about the extent of freedom of expression allotted to those who submit material to the MSU station.")

Actually, the words "damn" and "nigger" had indeed been used on WMSB.

Both words were contained in my play *Study in Color* which was telecast on July 12. This would seem to point up the fact that the words themselves were not the reasons for banning *Boy*, despite what was said publicly to that effect. Also, a taped program featuring James Baldwin had been shown on the station several weeks before, and Baldwin had used both words liberally in the course of his remarks.

Mr. Sherwood told the *Free Press* that *Boy* was the best of my three plays and that the station "probably objected to the dramatic intensity of the play. It's a very strong piece. A frightening piece." And I explained to the paper that *Boy* was written "to make the whites experience human pain. It cuts very deeply. I want to embarrass the whites. A lot of them must learn how the Negro suffers."

I pointed out that the words "damn" and "nigger" have been used on commercial television and criticized educational TV stations for not being more outspoken. *The Defenders, East Side/West Side, The Nurses* and other commercial programs have given extremely forthright treatment to racial situations. Educational television is not meant to be an ivory tower. A university educational television station has particular responsibilities in artistic and academic freedom, especially as related to areas of controversy. . . .

Reaction to the banning of *Boy* mounted swiftly. The *Michigan Chronicle*, a leading Negro newspaper, stated in a headline: "PLAY WOULD ONLY OFFEND 'THE WHITE BIGOT.'" The Ann Arbor *Michigan Daily* (July 24, 1964) criticized Mr. Hunter's "puritanical action" and went on to comment: "Certainly the station director cannot really suppose that he knows better than the writer which words are vital to a play and which are not. . . ."

Michigan State News, the MSU student newspaper, headlined its lead editorial on July 13: "'BOY' SUPPRESSION HIDES TRUTH." Its opinion was that "suppression of an educational play on race relations by an educational television station hardly seems conducive to educational enlightenment on this campus or in the State of Michigan. . . ."

The American Civil Liberties Union of Michigan (the Greater Lansing Branch) issued this protest to MSU: "The reasons for refusing to show a play dealing with race relations given by the head of Michigan State University's TV station reflect a shocking lack of sensitivity in dealing with controversial issues. . . . The Lansing community is indebted to Boyd for publicizing this action of censorship rather than remaining silent because two of his three plays were produced. The American Civil Liberties Union feels that Michigan State University should judge the merits of this play by the same standards used generally for the fine arts. . . . An author or playwright has the right to see his works presented in the form that he feels best expresses his ideas. A great university should be particularly sensitive to this problem and respect this right even though it may upset the sensitivities of some individuals. . . ."

But the station never presented the play. A member of the MSU Board of Trustees telephoned me and requested a copy of all data in my possession concerning the controversy, promising to bring up the matter at a meeting of the Board of Trustees. In fact, he said the full board would look at the tapes of *Boy* and the other two plays. However, the day of the meeting of the board passed, and the next, and the next. I never heard from the gentleman again. It is painful when truth is suppressed and justice is denied.

Writing in *Saturday Review* (August 15, 1964), Robert L. Shayon called *Study in Color* "a provocative exploration of racial attitudes" and commended it and *The Job* as "fresh, vital explorations with social bite and contemporary relevance." Then he commented on *Boy,* calling it "honest, uncompromising, and poignant." Mr. Shayon went on to say that the reasons offered for the censorship by WMSB spokesmen "on and off the record, simply don't wash, and one is justified in suspecting that the buck is being passed. . . . Such an affair disappoints educational television's friends, and it sets back the creative people in the field who want desperately to have their branch of the medium step out with courage and style and become meaningful in American life."

Shayon made this interesting observation, too: "Somebody was apparently afraid of someone, and the shock of having the timidity and dissimulation come from the academic community—where freedom of expression is presumably prized—undercuts the station's presentation of the two plays that were aired."

It seemed the incident was closed. I certainly assumed it was. But shortly thereafter, when I was in Switzerland giving lectures at an international conference there under the sponsorship of the World Council of Churches, the Associated Press telephoned me. Did I know I had been attacked by my bishop? No, I said, I did not.

In a newspaper column, the Rt. Rev. Richard S. Emrich, Bishop of Michigan, had written: "A newspaper article informed us that a play on racial justice, written by a clergyman, was banned because of its profanity by the radio [*sic*] station of a great university. Since the clergyman preaches and practices high and sensitive standards in race relations, it astounds me that his standards in language are so low. Rejecting the sin that divides man from man, it is astonishing that he is willing to offend men by accepting the vulgarity and profanity of the modern avant-garde stage."

So the *Boy* controversy had not ended. The *New York Times* headlined a story: "PRIEST IS REBUKED ON WORDS IN PLAY . . . EPISCOPAL BISHOP DEPLORES HIS PROFANITY IN DRAMA." . . .

The issues in the *Boy* controversy became so complex that the funda-

mental question—the role of educational television as related to controversy, the expression of new ideas and creative experimental work
—undoubtedly became obscured along the way. This role needs to be
examined carefully, painfully and honestly.

13 Other Media

Compared to newspapers, magazines, and broadcasting, movies and books have to be called minor. The average American sees only five or six films a year, and reads even fewer books. He spends infinitely more time in front of the TV set, listening to the radio, and reading his daily paper and his favorite magazine.

Interestingly enough, the biggest audience for both movies and books is made up of young people; they read the books in school and see the movies on their own time. "Adults" have relatively little to do with either one.

It was not always that way. In 1929, 110,000,000 people visited a movie theater every week. But by 1968, weekly movie attendance was down to 21,000,000. Many factors contributed to the decline—especially television. Throughout the 1950s and early 1960s, the film industry met the challenge of TV with multi-million-dollar spectaculars. It was a foolish tactic. Faced with the choice of an old movie on TV (for free) or a new movie in town (at three dollars a seat), the typical American preferred to stay home in his easy chair.

The people with the greatest natural inclination to get out of the house—teen-agers—were almost totally ignored by the movie magnates. But in the mid-1960s, a new generation of independent film makers came on the scene. The movies they produced ignored the old taboos as well as the old people. They spoke directly to the youth culture, and they revolutionized the industry. If film maker Haskell Wexler could bring in "Medium Cool" for under a million dollars for Paramount release, why should Paramount spend over $20 million on a bomb like "Paint Your Wagon"? By the end of the 1960s, the film industry had made up its mind. It bet its future on independent low-budget production and the American youth market.

The youth market supports the book industry in quite another way: by compulsion. Nearly half of all books published in the United States are texts or reference books, and they account for well over half of total sales. Needless to say, textbooks are read only by students, who seldom have any choice in the matter.

After textbooks, the largest categories in book publishing are mass-market paperbacks, juveniles, and book-club selections. The kind of book that sells only in bookstores (known as a "trade book") represents well under 10 percent of the publishing business.

Of course there are books that have changed the world—**Uncle Tom's Cabin,** for example, or Darwin's **Origin of the Species**. But even they did it indirectly. Fewer people have read these two since they were published than the number who watched "Bewitched" on TV last night. In the long term, books may well be the most important of the mass media. But in the everyday life of the average man, they are by far the least influential.

The wire service is a third mass medium of considerable importance, though it is seldom mentioned in lists of the media. Nearly every newspaper and many broadcast stations get the bulk of their nonlocal news from just two sources: the Associated Press and United Press International. If AP and UPI play a story up big, millions of Americans will find out about it. If AP and UPI ignore the story, so will the country.

The two wire services have thousands of clients of all sorts—big and little, domestic and foreign, leftist and rightist. The two main characteristics of the wires, speed and objectivity, both result from this diversity of clients. Every minute of every day, a wire service client somewhere has reached its deadline. Under pressure to get the story **now,** wire reporters make frequent errors of judgment and of fact. In an effort to keep everybody happy, they avoid interpretive journalism and news analysis, sticking closely to the who-what-where-when style of writing.

Objective or not, the wire services have no choice but to color the news. They **choose** the news. They decide which events to cover and which to ignore, which stories to put on the national wire and which to use only regionally. These decisions are made quickly and casually.

But as the selection that follows illustrates, they may have important repercussions.

THE M.B.I. and GOODBYE, M.B.I.

By A. J. LIEBLING

A couple of months ago, I had occasion to subscribe to twenty out-of-town newspapers, and the copies have been piling up in my office ever since. Though depressed at encountering the same syndicated features in one paper after another, I sometimes read four or five of these papers at a stretch when I have nothing better to do, and even when I have. It is like eating pistachio nuts from the shell—unrewarding but hard to stop once you have begun. . . .

Looking at the New Orleans *Times-Picayune* for November 14th, I found my attention caught by a story on the first page about something odd that was happening in the neighboring state of Mississippi, which the *Times-Picayune* considers to be in its circulation territory. The headline said:

POLICE POWERS
GRANTED WRIGHT

WHITTINGTON CHARGES FORCE
WOULD BE "GESTAPO"

I suppose "Gestapo" was the word that nailed me; we have all grown sensitive recently to stories about secret-police forces. The story, signed by W. F.

Minor, a *Times-Picayune* correspondent, began, "Over some protests of 'Gestapo' in both houses, the Mississippi Legislature today gave final passage to a far-reaching measure granting the Governor police power through investigators to suppress violence." Not having the least suspicion that Mississippi was having more than the usual amount of violence, I read on with some curiosity. "The legislation, key measure of seven bills presented to the extraordinary session which was convened Wednesday," the story continued, "was the outgrowth of recurring incidents of violence which have accompanied a six-month-old strike of drivers of the Southern (Trailways) Bus lines." Now, in any of the states in which I have resided long enough to learn local customs, a strike sufficiently bad to cause the governor to call a special session of the legislature to cope with it would be an impressive event, and I wondered why I had not read anything about this Mississippi rebellion before. I decided that I must have seen earlier stories in the New York papers but that I avoided reading them because of my resistance to any Southern dateline, and that I had

From the *New Yorker*, January 3, 1948, pp. 46–50, and February 7, 1948, pp. 51–55.   Reprinted in A. J. Liebling, *The Press* (New York: Ballantine Books, Inc., 1961), pp. 126–43.   Reprinted by permission of the estate of the author and its agent, James Brown Associates, Inc.   Copyright © 1948 by A. J. Liebling.   First published in *The New Yorker*.

forgotten that I had seen the headlines.

The police power that the legislature at Jackson had granted the Governor empowered him to create an organization that did not appear to be exactly like any state force with which I was familiar. It was to consist of investigators, appointed by and known only to him, who would have the power "to investigate and make arrests in crimes of violence or intimidation." "Regular" investigators were to post bonds of twenty-five hundred dollars with the Governor, Fielding L. Wright, and the Governor might also name any temporary, unbonded investigator he pleased. Among the six other proposed bills was one making it a jail offense for two or more persons to conspire to interfere with the operation of a transit line. Another made it a crime punishable by death to place a bomb in a bus, truck, or filling station, whether anybody was killed or not. Still another proposed a penalty of as much as five years in the penitentiary for anybody who had in his possession "dynamite caps, fuses, detonators, dynamite, nitroglycerine, explosive gas, or stink bombs," unless he was conducting a lawful business. . . .

It was difficult to believe that even such a superficial reader of newspapers as I could have missed all reference in the metropolitan dailies to what struck me—and, apparently, the editor of the *Times-Picayune*— as an important story. So I set a young man who occasionally helps me to checking through the New York newspapers for November to see if there were any stories on the Mississippi special session or on a notably violent strike preceding it. Meanwhile, I dived into the great mounds of nearly identical provincial newspapers that are gradually walling in my desk in search of the *Times-Picayune* for the few days before and after November 14th. The *Times-Picayune* of November 8th had a first-page story by Mr. Minor about an announcement Governor Wright had made to the effect that he would call a special session to ask "broader power and additional laws" to deal with the strike. The story also said that a brick had been thrown into the waiting room of a bus station and that a bus had been shot into but no one had been hit. I further learned that Mississippi already had a State Highway Patrol. An Associated Press dispatch run as a shirttail to the special story informed me that the striking union was the Amalgamated Association of Street Car, Railway, and Motor Coach Employees of America, A.F.L., and that the strike had been on since May 20th, when the company's contract with the union had expired. The *Times-Picayune* of November 12th said that Governor Wright had called the session on the ground that "the laws of the State had been trampled upon." A couple of legislators named Henley and Shanks had asked the Governor, "Is the legislature going to be convened every time there is a strike?" The *Times-Picayune* of November 13th carried a story on the Governor's specific legislative requests. It indicated that the members of the secret special force, to be called the Mississippi Bureau of Investigation, were to have the right to arrest without warrant any person whom they suspected of intent to interfere with a bus line, and to search him. The M.B.I. was to be provided with arms by the Governor. . . .

It seemed to me that this kind of legislation deserved prominent space in newspapers throughout the country, if only because of the sanguinary anarchy that must have reigned in Mississippi for months to justify anything like it. My state of mind, therefore, verged on astonishment when my file reader reported that in all the New York newspapers from the thirteenth through the sixteenth of November—including the *Daily Worker*, which surely would have welcomed the opportunity to play up this kind of news— he had found only one story about the Mississippi special session. That was a short piece on page 21 of the *Times* of Sunday, November 16th, under the headline "Bill to Curb Labor Fails in Mississippi." The lead said that the legislature had passed "all but one of six measures aimed at ending violence," and I noticed with amusement that the copyreader had based his head on the one bill that failed instead of the five that passed. The *Times* story had a Jackson dateline and was slugged "Special to the New York *Times*." . . .

I considered two possibilities: one, that I had misinterpreted the stories, although I could not understand why, if they really lacked weight, the

Times-Picayune should have devoted so much space to them; two, that the New York editors had simply never known about the yarn. . . . My helper phoned the Associated Press to ask what the people there knew about it. The answer was simple and direct: nothing. An official said that they hadn't seen anything of the story in the New York office. Two papers in Jackson, Mississippi, are members of the Associated Press, and so is the *Times-Picayune*, and presumably one or another of them sent out *something* on it, but not all stories put on the wire by Southern members come as far North as this. A news-association editor in Atlanta may decide that a story has only regional importance. An official at the United Press said he thought he remembered seeing the story, but he couldn't swear to it, and it would involve digging through bales of copy to check up on it. He said he didn't think it was worth while. He did ask the U.P. string man in Jackson, who said he had sent out five to six hundred words a day during the session but couldn't say how far up the line his stories had gone. I wired the U.P. bureau chief in Atlanta, but I got no answer. I know that if the story did get to Atlanta, the *Constitution* didn't use it, because I dug up the *Constitution* for the proper dates from my newspaper pile. . . .

The story of the M.B.I.'s creation and of the establishing of a new crime subject to capital punishment seems to me to have merited space in any American publication pretending to be a newspaper. (The prospect of forty-eight state Bureaus of Investigation, with armed personnel not of public record—a C.B.I. in Connecticut, an N.Y.B.I. here, an R.I.B.I. in Rhode Island—should have given the papers something to think about, too.) If editors the country over had this story in their offices and rejected it in favor of the fluffy wire stuff most of my specimen newspapers are filled with, then the national press is in a low state of health. . . . If the story never came over the press-association wires to where the editors could see it, or if it came in such feeble form that it could not be properly evaluated, somebody ought to begin mending that fine-mesh news net that the heads of press associations are always bragging about. From where I sit, that net looks more like a toothless rake.

A few weeks ago, I described at considerable length in this department how the daily press handled—or, with few exceptions, didn't handle—the story of some laws recently enacted at a special session of the Mississippi legislature primarily as a means of maintaining order during a strike against a bus company in that state. . . .

A letter I received from a man named Talbot Patrick a couple of days after the publication of my piece nicely supported my point. Mr. Patrick, who is editor and publisher of the *Evening Herald* of Rock Hill, South Carolina (population 15,009), wrote:

Your report on this case should jolt wire-service staff members out of a sort of hypnosis in which, while handling masses of words in a routine way, they lose alertness for everything except surface accuracy and a chance for speed. A jolt like this forces an appreciation of the meaning to human lives of ideas behind the words they handle—and what makes up human life is the important part of the medium—and smaller-size American daily newspapers.

The press associations are miracles of modern mechanics. No wonder that sometimes the servants of the machine fail to think through, beyond, past the machine and the radio stations and the newspapers, to the men and women who work and eat and worry and try to go forward.

From Mr. Patrick's letter, I assumed that the *Evening Herald,* although a member of the Associated Press, had not received much, if any, coverage on the Mississippi Bureau of Investigation, or, as it has since come to be known, the M.B.I. . . .

Both the Associated Press, which is a cooperative organization of 2,398 member newspapers and radio stations, with, in addition, 1,490 subscribers, and the United Press, its chief rival, which is a privately owned enterprise selling news to 2,947 customers, have permanent bureaus at Jackson, the capital of Mississippi. Before the appearance of my piece on the Mississippi Bureau of Investigation, an Associated Press editor here in New York told me that he could not remember having seen anything come over the wires about those laws. Apparently, though, something did. Paul Mickelson, the A.P.'s general news editor, has since informed me that the A.P. man in Jackson sent out a pretty fair three-hundred-and-forty-word story on the night of November 13th, immediately following the passage of the legislation in question. This, the crucial story of the session, went out to Southern morning papers. (If Patrick, in South Carolina, did not receive it, that would be because his paper is an evening one.) The press-association empires are divided into regional satrapies, and to reach New York, for wider distribution, copy out of Jackson must be passed upon successively by bureaus in New Orleans and Atlanta. The New Orleans and Atlanta men waved the November 13th story on, and it came into the Associated Press main office, in New York, that night. Here, however, nobody thought much of it, and it was cut down to two hundred words, losing its moderate punch in the process. It was then, for some mysterious reason, sent out on a subsidiary circuit serving only newspapers west of New York City. It was not sent to newspapers here or in several other large Eastern cities at all.

After the appearance in this department of my somewhat bewildered speculations, the Baltimore *Sun*, an important member of the A.P., wired the association's New York office asking why it hadn't received a full account of the Mississippi situation and requesting that it be supplied with one. The New York office, endeavoring to comply, got after the Atlanta, New

Orleans, and Jackson A.P. men, who must have been astonished at the sudden flareup of interest in the story after a month and a half of apparent unconcern. Jackson sent out a quite good six-hundred-word story on January 3rd, telling about the M.B.I. and adding that the legislature would meet in regular session on January 6th and that Governor Wright was now saying that he didn't want his secret-police force any more and was willing to swap it for some other kind of police department. . . .

The whole incident was recently reviewed, from the A.P. point of view, in a report to the publisher-members of the organization. A copy of this document, passed along to me by one of my more adept operatives, is here quoted, entirely without permission:

The fact is we booted general service delivery of a significant news story, last Nov. 13, reporting actions by the Mississippi state legislature, featuring establishment of a secret police force.

The legislature's action was a climax of developments in Mississippi connected with a protracted and violent strike of bus drivers. From Jackson, Miss., in the night report of Nov. 13, we did transmit a comprehensive news story, but it was (a) transmitted in full only on the south regional (GGG) wire, and (b) cut so sharply on the west wire (BBB) relay that the really significant news details were lost. On top of these misjudgments, we slipped up entirely on relay to New York City members, and failed to discover the actual facts of this foulup in time to tell *The New Yorker,* which quizzed us.

All of this is the subject of intensive staff review, for object lesson purposes. . . . It is particularly a lesson to control bureaus (in this case, New Orleans, Atlanta, and New York) not to permit even the crush of an extraordinarily big news day (which Nov. 13 was) to sidetrack or overlook the national significance of news having its roots in a regional situation.

The United Press was less contrite about its handling of the M.B.I. story. I was told by U.P. editors in New York that their man in Jackson had sent out five-hundred-word stories to Southern clients every day of the legislature's special session, but they were, regrettably, unable to show me copies of any of them. They did, however, produce the parts of them that had been sent along by the Atlanta bureau for their Round Robin, or main trunk wires. These amounted to a couple of hundred words a day, sent in scrappy, fragmentary form— "first leads," "second leads," and "adds" of a few words each, none of which could have given an editor who was not familiar with the situation much idea of what was happening. There was no mention, for instance, of the peculiarly anonymous character of the M.B.I. A woman who acts as a news editor of a New England radio station that receives U.P. service has written me that she "used several stories but finally gave up as they became more complicated and bizarre. You can't do as much explaining on radio news as in a newspaper

. . . so the Mississippi-type stories are just a headache." After I looked over the U.P. stuff out of Atlanta, I saw the lady's point. The lead on one bit read, "Efforts to modify or expand a bill which would give the Governor special investigators with police powers were defeated in the Senate. . . ." The impact of this sort of thing, with a Jackson, Mississippi, dateline, on an editor in another part of the country would obviously be fairly feeble. The news and telegraph editors of the *Herald Tribune,* to whom I spoke before writing my first story on the case, could not remember having seen any of the U.P. material. It even made no impression at *PM,* always on the alert for the liberty-in-peril type of story.

Unfortunately, most of the belated interest in the M.B.I. story, while gratifying, has nothing to do with the point I originally wanted to make. The newspapers have by now given considerable publicity to the threat implicit in an organization like the Mississippi Bureau of Investigation; they probably have bolstered, if they did not inspire, Governor Wright's decision that he can get along without it. . . . What impresses, and depresses, me, though, is that by looking through a few old newspapers I was able to find a pretty big story that the main organs of news distribution had completely muffed. I can't help wondering how often stories of general importance appear in full solely in local papers and get out to the rest of the country only after they have been compressed into insignificance. This reflection leads me to another, still more depressing: I wonder how many important stories never get into the newspapers at all. The American press makes me think of a gigantic, supermodern fish cannery, a hundred floors high, capitalized at eleven billion dollars, and with tens of thousands of workers standing ready at the canning machines, but relying for its raw material on an inadequate number of handline fishermen in leaky rowboats. At the point of contact with the news, the vast newsgathering organizations are usually represented either by a couple of their own harried reporters, averaging, perhaps, twenty-two years and eleven months old, or by a not too perceptive reporter on a small-town paper whose version of an event, written up for his employer, may or may not be passed on to the wire services by someone in the office. Not all the newspaper owners' towers of masonry, with their ingenious insides, like the Daily News Building, or all the tons of newsprint covered with red and black ink and pictures of women jumping out of windows can add anything to the quality of what these reporters regard as significant.

Press-association reporters are warned when they start in of the necessity for keeping down the volume of news and sending only what a fairly large number of newspapers are likely to use. This sometimes seems to mean a story about a dog that refuses to leave its dead master's newsstand or a child who has swallowed a whistling teakettle. I do not doubt that November 13th was an extraordinarily big news day, as the A.P. report to its members says it was, but I could not help noting that the Chicago *Sun* and the St. Louis *Post-Dispatch* of November 14th both carried a two-hundred-word A.P. story datelined College Park, Georgia, about a woman who, upon being fined seven dollars for driving past a stop sign, insisted on serving seven days in jail instead of paying, and made such a nuisance of herself that they finally let her go. This must have been part of the news that so crowded the A.P.'s wires that the M.B.I. story had to be cut down to two hundred words and incoherence.

14 Advertising and Public Relations

Advertising is the all-important connection between the mass media and the world of commerce. The relationship is symbiotic. Without advertising, neither the media nor the industrial establishment could survive in the form we know them today.

American business spends over $20 billion a year on advertising, most of it in the mass media. The purpose of every ad is to persuade the public to buy something that the advertiser has to sell—a product, a service, a political candidate, or even a point of view. A successful ad is an ad that sells.

Most ads in the media make some attempt to win a bigger share of the existing market; they urge the reader, listener, or viewer to switch brands. But this sort of competitive advertising is only a small part of the picture. If the only way a manufacturer could earn a dollar was by wooing it away from some other manufacturer, America's gross national product would be at a standstill. Industry grows by creating new consumer needs—for wigs and cigarettes, for power lawnmowers and deodorants, for fur coats and aluminum cans. The overarching goal of nearly all advertising is to get the consumer to consume.

The media depend on advertising just as heavily as the rest of big business. Television and radio earn all of their money from advertising, which fills up some 20 percent of the total air time. Newspapers and magazines earn well over three-quarters of their income from advertising, which occupies roughly 60 percent of the available space. Of all the mass media, only books and movies are completely independent of advertisers.

In return for advertising revenue, the mass media give up some portion of their independence. Certain facts (embarrassing to advertisers) are not reported; certain issues (offensive to consumers) are not treated; certain philosophies (dangerous to materialism) are not expressed. It may be a good trade for the media. But the public also loses the advantages of media independence—and gains little in return. In fact, the public pays for the ads. The average family of four spends over $50 a year in increased product costs for television advertising alone.

Public relations has essentially the same goals as advertising—to "sell" a company, product, ideology, or whatever to the public. The difference is one of method. Advertising men are forced to work in the open; the audience recognizes a paid advertisement and responds accordingly. Public-relations men, on the other hand, work in secret. They plan stunts to be covered as news, write press releases to be printed as news, and generally do their best to see to it that their client looks as good as possible in the mass media. The handiwork of a successful public-relations man is almost never identified as such.

The job of the advertising and public-relations industries is persuasion. It is a hard job, and they do it well. By and large, they also do it ethically, at least according to their own standards. But ethical or not, the professional persuaders make us nervous. They are too skilled, too powerful, and too devious to be studied with equanimity.

For many years, the Dodge automobile has been associated with dependability, maturity, and age. This was a good reputation to have in the 1950s, but by the mid-1960s the Dodge makers felt a need for a "younger" image. And so, in 1965, the Dodge Rebellion was born. The selection that follows traces the development of the Dodge Rebellion advertising campaign. Largely as a result of that campaign, a good percentage of the readers of this book probably drove to school this morning in a Dodge.

No One Gets Hurt in This Rebellion, But Dodge Auto Gets a Swinging Image

Pam Austin is a rebel with a cause: youth. That's what she gives Dodge, a car long associated with the term "dependability." Now dependability is a nice word, but for some it had begun to conjure up the wrong image at a time when half the U.S. population is under 30. Dependability can project to the more switched-on among us a picture of a middle-aged dentist driving to the grocery store in Oskaloosa to buy Wonder bread, Jello and Geritol for a wife he refers to as "mother." That sterling but not swinging image was smashed forever when Miss Austin donned her go-go boots, turtle-neck sweater and stretch pants to launch the Dodge rebellion.

According to John F. Bergin, VP-creative director and plans-board chairman at BBDO (agency for Dodge cars and trucks), there has been "a significant shift" in attitudes toward Dodge since the campaign began with a cannon blast in the fall of 1965. (The initial commercials were slotted in World Series coverage to introduce the 1966 Dodge line.) "Dodge suddenly emerged as a younger, more exciting, more appealing car in image studies," he says. "At the same time it hasn't really lost any of the valuable aspects of its reputation as a substantial performer."

Bergin stands in awe of the marketing phenomenon that youth represents today. "There's never been such a unified, homogeneous mass of people in the same age range, and with rather similar education, in simi-

From *Television*, 24, no. 2 (February, 1967), 34–35, 43. Reprinted by permission.

lar economic circumstances and with enormous, unbelievable marketing power," he says. "It represents almost every product's prime target."

Bergin had this target in mind when he went to Detroit to attend the unveiling of Dodge's '66 models. These debuts, he says, are handled very seriously with an audience of insiders and the cars concealed behind drapes. As the drapes are pulled aside, the spectators applaud for each car and cheer its designer. "This was my first experience at this kind of event. I'm not a car buff, but these cars really dazzled me. I thought they represented a real shift away from what might have been thought of as a stodgy Dodge, a shift to almost 'custom' cars. It struck me right then and there that they were designed to give you a big kick. They would make it fun even to drive to the corner drug store for a pack of cigarettes. As I said later in a rationale for our campaign, the new Dodge reflected a rebellion in driver attitude."

After the unveiling, Bergin, along with the copy chiefs from BBDO's Detroit office, headed a creative team that went to a secret, out-of-season motor lodge in St. Claire, Mich., which they called Shangri-La. There were some 24 agency people in the team, made up largely of artists and writers. The aim was to generate a volume of ideas for the Dodge campaign, just as many professional photographers nowadays will take hundreds of pictures on the supposition that at least a handful will be excellent. Bergin says "everybody went off like monks" to think. There were plenty of sharpened pencils around. The first thing Bergin put down on his drawing pad was an Uncle Sam type poster bearing the legend: "The Dodge rebellion wants you."

The word "rebellion," to Bergin, neatly encompasses two concepts. "Its primary motive was to get the young on our side," he says. "The spirit of youthful rebellion is about as traditional as Christmas. It also ties into the market itself: People were demanding more power, more luxury features, more personality in their automobiles. There was a period when Detroit went overboard for the stripped-down, plain-Jane kind of car. You can almost say people rebelled."

Some 100 ideas for advertising the 1966 Dodge came out of Shangri-La. These were narrowed to six finalists and the client ultimately chose the rebellion approach. It differs from the one-year slogans that Detroit turns out with as much facility as it turns out cars, Bergin says, by representing "a marketing posture." (The current campaign for Mustang also conceivably shares this trait, Bergin says.)

The rebellion idea went through much pretesting and some modification before it saw the light of day as a finished commercial. The major problem was to make clear that this was designed to be, in Bergin's words, "a fun rebellion, not a bloody rebellion." Out of this problem came the notion of having the rebellion led by a blonde girl who, if she does blow up a bridge, does it by misadventure. Before she was thought of, suggested commercials simply showed young, fresh people driving Dodges. But the agency decided that using an inept blonde would take the onus off some of the negative aspects of rebellion by making it humorous. The campaign went through some six presentations at various levels of the Dodge management and its parent corporation, Chrysler.

"Each time, the agency explained that what it was presenting might seem to be an almost revolutionary move that could run into some criticism and flak," Bergin says. "But after the showings, someone usually said: 'I don't see anything that scares me. Go ahead.' Of course there were people on the fringes who said the campaign would stir up unrest at a time when there was rebellion all over the world. But the public is never as nervous about advertising as it's expected to be. It understands this is a joke."

Kong Wu, a TV art director at BBDO, drew up a series of storyboards in color from which the agency made 16-mm test commercials. "The girl he drew was literally a picture of the girl, Pam Austin, we later cast for the commercials. She was discovered by Don Schwab, TV producer in our Hollywood office, playing a part (blonde entertainer with a heart of gold) in a segment of *My Three Sons*. The thing that dazzled everybody—the writers, television director, the client—was she was the exact person drawn on the storyboard. She got instant approval."

During the first year of the campaign, another girl, New York model Connie Snow, posed for the print ads while Miss Austin did the commercials. This year, for the sake of greater unity, Miss Austin is doing both the print and television campaigns. However, this year she is assisted by stunt girls, while last year she did it all herself.

All the commercials are done in Hollywood, where the weather is right and where they know how to rig for difficult derring-do. VPI did the first group of commercials and Columbia Screen Gems others in the series. Eighteen were turned out for the 1966 campaign and the same number for operation 1967. The format changed a little this year. Originally, whatever was going to happen to Pam happened in the first few seconds and then the commercial focused on the car. "This year," says Bergin, "we use one of the devices of the old-time movie serial. We open with Pam getting into trouble and as the trouble develops we freeze the frame. Then we cut to the car and then unfreeze to resume with her. You've got to stay with it to see how she came out of it. At the same time we're selling the hell out of the car."

For the 23-year-old Miss Austin, married to Hollywood public relations man Guy F. McElwaine and mother of a young son, the campaign has paid off. She got a handsome raise last year, and although her pilot for a projected TV series, *Perils of Pauline*, didn't make it, Universal-

International, which owns it, is expanding it for feature distribution. Trailers for the movie tie in with the Dodge rebellion theme, which makes BBDO and client happy.

"We find an occasional customer here and there who doesn't like Pam Austin," Bergin says, "but the giant majority does, and that happily enough includes women. Here you have a little gal with clear and obvious sex appeal who is fresh enough and charming enough to appeal to women as well as the major car buyers, men. And it's quite a trick when you can get women watching car commercials."

When A. C. Thomson, manager of Dodge car advertising, announced that the rebellion theme would be renewed for the 1967 cars with an increased budget, he reported that a study last April disclosed that public recognition of the theme had risen above 71%. He also said that this recognition ranged from 24% to 64% better than for the campaigns of competing cars.

More successfully than many dowagers, Dodge has dropped a few years from its image.

PART FOUR
COVERAGE

15 Coverage
of Government

The heroic, hard-drinking "typical" newspaperman of the movies has a lot of flaws, but in at least one way he is ideal. His attitude toward government officials is magnificently suspicious and uncompromising. Inevitably, he winds up the third reel with a crusading exposé on the abuse of public trust by a public official—and to hell with the repercussions. This sort of attitude is the basis for all good coverage of government. Critic William L. Rivers terms it "the adversary relationship."

In the real world, as opposed to the movies, the adversary relationship is rare. There are many reasons.

1. **Friendship.** Most government reporters are specialists; they cover the Justice Department or City Hall or the Pentagon full time. Specialization has many advantages, but one big disadvantage: the reporter is likely to become a close personal friend of his news sources. And friendly reporters seldom write embarrassing articles about their friends.

2. **Sympathy.** It is good for a newsman to understand the official's point of view, but if he understands it too well for too long he may come to accept it. For this reason most New York newspapers impose a mid-season shuffle on the reporters who cover the Yankees and the Mets. Such a shuffle would do wonders for government coverage.

3. **Dependence.** Government reporters depend on their sources for

everything from front-page scoops to last-paragraph quotes. They are understandably reluctant to do anything to offend them. And nothing offends a source as fast as a muckraking article.

4. **Alliance.** Many a reporter starts out covering a government official and winds up working for him—unofficially. Washington is full of such part-time officials; they draft bills, guide press conferences, suggest handouts, and otherwise join in the process of governing. On the local level, reporters may wind up moonlighting as press agents for their sources. Their reporting, of course, suffers.

5. **Complexity.** The time when most of the news corps understood most of the news is long past. Today a government reporter must write about the intricacies of spaceflight, inflation, the arms race, air pollution, urban renewal, and many similar topics. To make sense of these issues, he relies heavily on the help of government experts. It is hard to be aggressive and independent when covering a story you do not understand to start with.

6. **Secrecy.** Despite the existence of laws guaranteeing "open access" to most government meetings and government documents, much of the governing process still goes on in secret. Even a skilled reporter may dig for the truth and fail to unearth it.

7. **News management.** Nearly half the public-relations men in the country are employed by government. Their job is to manage the news in the best interests of their employer. Most public-relations men are good at their job—making the reporter's job that much harder.

8. **Understaffing.** The Washington press corps is composed of more than 2,000 full-time reporters, the cream of the journalistic crop. Even so, a great deal of federal news (especially from the "minor" executive agencies) receives only cursory attention from overworked newsmen. The problem is much more severe on the state and local levels, where a handful of reporters must cover the entire apparatus of government.

9. **Speed.** The faster a reporter works, the less thorough and accurate he is likely to be. Yet all the news media put a tremendous premium on speed. The wire services are the biggest offenders in this area; five minutes after a Supreme Court decision is announced, AP and UPI have a summary on the wires. Often it is not an adequate summary.

10. **Civic boosterism.** Local publishers and broadcasters are inevitably leaders of their communities. They belong to the right country clubs and are active in the chamber of commerce and the Red Cross drive. They are reluctant to do or say anything that would offend their friends or blacken the reputation of their town.

Several of these factors figure in the selection that follows, an angry account of an exposé that never got printed.

SUN–TIMES KILLS EXPOSÉ OF SWIBEL RENEWAL DEAL

By CHRISTOPHER CHANDLER

There is strong circumstantial evidence that the bidding was rigged on the city's $250,000,000 Madison-Canal urban renewal project.

Charles Swibel, head of the Chicago Housing Authority, protégé of Mayor Daley and owner of some property in the renewal area, won the bid last December under highly unusual circumstances.

Every facet of the project, from Swibel's lucrative partnership agreement to the strange bidding procedures, points to the workings of a very sophisticated form of graft involving top men in the Daley administration.

How does a newspaper handle a potentially explosive story of this kind? The *Sun-Times* took the matter very seriously. Starting last July, there were conferences on the story involving Bailey K. Howard, president of the newspaper division of Field Enterprises; Emmett Dedmon, vice president and editorial director of the Field papers; James Hoge, editor of the *Sun-Times;* Ralph Otwell, managing editor; the paper's libel lawyers; and Swibel himself.

The story was killed once, resurrected, and finally, in the first week of October, killed again.

Whatever the reason, major obstacles were certainly not apparent when the story first came to light.

I stumbled on the story last June, while working on an investigation of the city's prefab housing program. Swibel and Martin Bartling, a vice president of the Chicago-based U.S. Gypsum Company, appeared to be jointly running the program, which seemed an unusual arrangement for a publicly-funded venture.

Checking around on the relationship between the two men, I ran into a new civic watchdog group called Businessmen for the Public Interest, which had been exploring this same relationship. BPI had discovered a partnership agreement in the files of the Securities and Exchange Commission which outlined an unbelievably good deal for both Swibel and Bartling. They would make tens of millions of dollars as partners in the Madison-Canal urban renewal project, without making any investment, without performing any duties, and without incurring any obligations.

A quick telephone check showed that the losing bidders on the project believed it was rigged. Some architects were outraged at the Department of Urban Renewal's procedures on the bid. Other developers thought the project looked phony.

Hoge's first reaction was en-

From *Chicago Journalism Review*, 2, no. 11 (November, 1969), 3–6. Reprinted by permission.

thusiastic. "This is an obvious payoff," he said, when shown the section of the partnership agreement which gave Swibel 12.5 per cent plus $100,000 a year for ten years "beginning upon the acceptance of the partnership as the successful bidder."

Hoge assigned two reporters, Ray Brennan and Basal Talbott Jr., to help me out on the investigation. He was leaving for a vacation, but he suggested we go with the first story the following Sunday.

Howard, informed by Hoge that a story was in the works, summoned me to his office on the seventh floor and said, "Let's go after him."

At this point the story had top priority.

On Thursday, July 31, Brennan, Talbott and I discussed our approach to the story in a brief huddle. Brennan, the most experienced investigative reporter at the *Sun-Times*, had interviewed one of the losing bidders and their attorneys, and had a signed letter detailing the ways in which the Swibel bid failed to meet the specifications for the Madison-Canal project.

Talbott had contacted architects on the losing bid who had at one time planned to demand an investigation by the American Institute of Architects, citing the DUR's failure to appoint an architectural review committee. He was particularly impressed with the fact that other Chicago architects told him they had shied away from the Madison-Canal project from the beginning because of suspicions of a fix.

I had obtained a copy of an anonymous letter, written to the *Chicago Daily News*, which predicted—before the bids were submitted—that Swibel's group would win because the whole renewal project was a setup.

We still didn't have a witness, or proof that the bid was fixed. But everything pointed in that direction. The businessmen's group was planning to file a conflict-of-interest lawsuit against Swibel the following week, and to send at some point a memorandum to the State Housing Board calling for an investigation.

We worked out the following strategy: The story in Sunday's paper would simply lay out the partnership agreement. Brennan reasoned that people would be interested in reading about the fact that Swibel, a close associate of the mayor and head of a city agency, stood to make millions on a city project. A second story would be based on the BPI petition to the State Housing Board, which we could arrange to have mailed Saturday, and a third piece would be on the lawsuit. Then there would be follow-up stories on questions about the bidding procedures, other agencies joining in the investigation, and developments on what would by then be an ongoing story.

I wrote the first story that Thursday night, laying out the terms of the partnership in a flat, impartial way. Brennan and Talbott both read it Friday morning and approved. Each made suggestions on reworking the first page to make it more dramatic. Brennan was going to write a sidebar story on Swibel.

Talbott was off that day, and Brennan was busy elsewhere, so I went in alone to see the editors and lawyers.

The initial reaction of Ralph Otwell, managing editor, and Ken Towers, assistant editor, was good. "Hell of a story," said Towers. Otwell noted, as we headed toward the conference with the libel attorneys, that we would have to have the story approved that day, since our lawyer was about to go on vacation.

There followed a confused, confusing three-hour session in the office of William P. Steven, a Field vice president.

The attorneys read the story carefully, cross-examined me on the material, pored over a copy of the partnership agreement, and debated Illinois conflict of interest law. Finally they left, saying that while the story was not libelous, Swibel had apparently not violated any conflict of interest laws. That tended to confuse things since the story did not allege any conflict of interest.

The mood of the group began to change. No one present had ever written an investigative story. As they thought about it, each began to imagine how such stories should be written.

Steven was impressed with the way the *Wall Street Journal* had done a detailed, months-in-preparation profile of the New York newspaper circulation king. Otwell thought we should make the first story harder-hitting, and lay out the major charges right away. Towers seemed increasingly nervous, repeatedly saying we had to contact Swibel again

for any additional rebuttal, that there should be more Swibel rebuttal higher up in the story and more regularly throughout, and that we needed more time to do a more careful job. He suggested we put the whole matter over until the following Monday.

I argued that the story was not libelous, that everything was set to go on subsequent stories, and that I could make any necessary changes in plenty of time for the Sunday paper.

Otwell was the man who made the decision, saying we would go back to work on it Monday. I said I was not willing to delay my vacation to work on a story that had no clear prospect of being used, and we left it at that. The material would be turned over to Ray Brennan for any rewriting that might be necessary.

I was convinced then that the story would not see print, but I wasn't sure why. The libel lawyer would be out of town the following week, which did not bode well. Still, Brennan is highly respected, and might be able to do something. I left a note for Brennan saying the story was now in his hands, and wishing him luck with it.

The following Monday, August 4, there was another meeting, even stranger than Friday's. I had to come into the office to get some papers from my desk before leaving on vacation, and was asked to stay, on overtime, for a meeting with Swibel and Bartling.

Emmett Dedmon had returned from his vacation and presided at the meeting in the editorial conference room. Present were Steven, Otwell, Towers and myself.

Before the guests arrived Dedmon launched into an angry denunciation of the story. He said it was "naive." He said the *Sun-Times* would "look silly" if we ran a story like that, displaying our ignorance of the workings of high finance. His voice rose as he talked. He said it was unethical to quote anonymous sources (although the only nameless sources were a "spokesman" for the BPI and an investment analyst for a brokerage firm). Dedmon warned:

"The *Sun-Times* will never run a story like this as long as you and I are both on this newspaper, do you understand that, Chandler?"

I replied that I understood what he was saying, but that I was not sure he had all the facts about the background of the story.

This discussion was cut short by the arrival of Bartling and Swibel. They proceeded to answer questions in a very friendly, lengthy fashion.

An investigator for the BPI called that night and I told him that the story was not going to run in the *Sun-Times*, in any form. He asked if I thought they should try to get some of the material printed in another paper, and I said they should. I even suggested a few reporters who might be interested.

That Thursday, Mike Royko ran a column in the *Daily News* about how profitable the Madison-Canal deal was going to be for Swibel. He based it on the partnership agreement and an interview with Swibel, and he managed to pin Swibel down on how much his interest was worth—$50,000,000 or so.

Royko says that his editor inquired about the column while he was working on it. But Royko's copy is not edited.

That column is, to date, the only story to appear in any newspaper on the Madison-Canal deal. But there was another whole laborious episode to be played out at the *Sun-Times*.

Hoge called me in to his office in the first week in September, when we had both returned from vacation, and said the *Sun-Times* was prepared to go ahead with a story on Swibel. He thought the original story was very good, he said, and it would have run had he been in town. He was apologetic for the way it had been handled. He said Dedmon was "contrite."

I should go back to work on it, Hoge said, and gather material for a new lead (since Royko had already had the column on the partnership agreement) and then "we will lay it all out."

I spent the week trying to bolster the story. It appeared that a competing bid, offered by Allied Products, Inc., a large industrial firm, was superior to the Swibel bid. The fact that Bartling's name did not appear on the bid documents was a clear violation of the specifications for the bidding. Real estate executives said they knew of no case in which the Department of Urban Renewal had decided on a bid in such a short time. Swibel had lied to me about Bartling's role as a partner.

But by the following week,

Hoge had become a little more cautious about the story. In a brief conference in his office, Hoge explained that for "both internal and external" reasons we would have to make it clear why we were going into this matter in such detail. "It shouldn't look like a vendetta," he said. He suggested that I focus the story on the urban renewal law and problems with the urban renewal system, and use the Madison-Canal project to illustrate these problems.

I submitted the story, written as he asked, on September 17. It was a very detailed account focused on the "lack of safeguards" in the city's new system for urban renewal.

Two weeks later Hoge stopped by my desk and mentioned that the story was "all right with me" and that he was sending it on to his superiors.

In early October I was summoned into Hoge's office on another matter. After that was cleared up I asked about the status of the Swibel story.

"I'll be frank with you," he said, locating his copy on his desk top.

"I don't think you have a story here."

Well, that was it. We discussed the merits of the story for some time, but the subject had become academic. Hoge's main argument was that I failed to show anything had transpired that had hurt the public interest.

"What if Swibel builds a good project out there?" he asked.

I am sure that *Sun-Times* executives will argue that I am a disgruntled employee who didn't have as much as he claimed, just as former *Daily News* reporter Don Barlett and former *Sun-Times* reporter Sandy Smith were supposed to have not really had much on important politicians when they quit in a rage.

I think there were three main reasons for the scuttling of the Swibel story.

Swibel enjoys a special status at the *Sun-Times* because of his friendship with Emmett Dedmon. The two men were neighbors in South Shore and cooperated to bring the South Shore school plan into being. Swibel aided the *Sun-Times* on its McCormick Place crusade. In the summer of 1967 I wrote a three part series on public housing which was killed because of this friendship (after three rewritings and lengthy confusion) and I would not knowingly have entered into another fracas about a Swibel story. What was confusing in this case was that Hoge and Howard seemed prepared to go ahead with it.

The second reason is more general. The *Sun-Times* is not a "muckraking" kind of a newspaper, and I don't believe it has ever broken a story questioning the activities of a prominent Chicago civic leader. I told Hoge last spring that the *Sun-Times* could break a series of scandals and make a difference in this city if we really went after them. Hoge replied, "I will print anything you come up with, even if it means my job," so again it looked like precedents might be set. On the other hand he declined to assign anyone to do investigative reporting. The Swibel story came up accidentally.

Finally there is a structural problem at the *Sun-Times* and probably at many other papers. Increasingly, important decisions are made above the level of editor. The Field papers have a publisher, a president, and four vice presidents who are to varying degrees involved in editorial policy. The editor of a Field paper no longer can decide any matter of important policy, and how these decisions are made seems to be increasingly remote.

I told Hoge at that last conference that at least I had gained some insight into the workings of urban renewal and city government. I could have added, "and the workings of one large newspaper."

16   Coverage of Crimes and Demonstrations

The favorite topic of the American mass media, bar none, is crime and violence. The average newspaper or broadcast station may or may not cover a new city ordinance or a school-bond issue. But a bank robbery, an assault, or (gulp—hold the presses) a rape-murder is almost guaranteed extensive play. For one thing, crime news helps boost circulation. For another, it is ridiculously easy to cover. A reporter need only sit at a desk in the police station, chat with his buddies on the force, and wait for the story to walk in the door—in handcuffs.

This sort of coverage has many dangers. At best, it is a waste of time and space. Perhaps if the media reported the sociology of crime, or white-collar crime, or organized crime, massive attention might be justified. But a barroom brawl simply is not as important to the community as a school-bond issue.

Certainly there are cases where crime news is of such monumental social importance that it must be published. (One such case was the assassination of President Kennedy in 1963.) But most of the time crime reporting does the accused some harm and nobody any good. Sensational crime news may actually be bad for society as well, creating a "climate of violence"—though this allegation is as yet unproved.

Even in cases where the amount of crime news is justified, the style and content of that news may be objectionable.   Since crime reporters work hand in glove with the police, crime stories inevitably favor the official point of view.   The facts of the arrest are well covered.   But the motives of the accused, the underlying causes of the crime, the protestations of innocence, and the eventual acquittal are not.

This is often true even for the most important sorts of "crime" stories —riots, demonstrations, and civil disturbances.   The practical problems of riot coverage are enormous, but the biggest problem of all is balance. Which reporter does your local city editor pick to cover a violent demonstration on campus?   The education writer, who knows (or should know) the issues?   Or the police reporter, who knows how to keep tabs on the number of arrests?   Most of the time it is the police reporter.   And the resulting article reflects his special expertise.

In the selection that follows, Nathan Blumberg of the University of Montana uses the adjective "orthodox" to describe the attitude of the media toward civil disturbances.   Using as an example the 1968 antiwar march on the Pentagon, Blumberg documents his view that serious challenges to the status quo are unlikely to be treated fairly in the press. The orthodox media, says Blumberg, rely heavily on official sources, stress action and violence, and ignore underlying issues.   The indictment may be overstated—the media were hardly orthodox in their coverage of the 1968 Democratic nominating convention in Chicago.   But it is more accurate than most editors and reporters like to admit.

NATHAN B. BLUMBERG

A Study of the "Orthodox" Press: The Reporting of Dissent

It is not enough to suggest that one of the most significantly misreported news stories of the past three years has been the growth and depth of disaffection toward the American commitment in Vietnam.   The imperative next question must be: Why did it happen this way?   One probable

From *Montana Journalism Review*, 1968, pp. 2–9.   Reprinted by permission.

answer is that it always has happened this way and we have been looking at the history of the American press through an unfocused micro-
scope.

A curiously consistent thread runs through the pattern of press performance from the time of John Peter Zenger to today. The historians
and the critics have examined and diagnosed the press as if it were a
monolithic structure, when the historical fact is that we always have had
a press that was essentially satisfied with the government and generally
satisfactory to the government (which could be called an "orthodox"
press) and at the same time another press that sought to change the
status quo (which in the current sense could be termed an "underground"
press). . . .

So long as the mass media are dealing with political parties, groups,
movements or individuals seeking reform or change within the explicit
structure of the current society, they generally perform with fairness and
objectivity. But let someone or something advocate a fundamental
change in the status quo—opposition to a war or a contemplated war, the
abolition of slavery, wobblyism, communism, socialism, anarchism, fas-
cism—and the press moves over to join those in political or economic
power who also have a stake in the continuation of things the way they
are.

Thus it should come as no surprise that the mass media of information have been incredibly slow—and still are—in reporting the revolutionary temper that racks the Negro ghettos. . . . Similarly, hippies—
who do not drink booze, are nonviolent and insist on structuring their
lives outside the demands of a conformist society—most often are sub-
jected to reports ranging from bristling hatred to amused contempt. The
members of the New Left and other revolutionaries can count on distortions of their views and actions by an uncomprehending press (or, if you
will, a press that on occasion comprehends only too well). And it is not
only members of the radical left who generally receive the back of the
hand from the mass media; the Ku Klux Klan, the American Nazi party
and the John Birch Society similarly have legitimate complaints that they
rarely receive objective treatment in news or interpretive stories.

In much the same way the mass media, wittingly or not, have minimized the nature and extent of dissent from the war policies of the government. It is essential to recognize that dissent has come to be regarded
as a threat to the existing order because it has moved out of the halls of
the Capitol, where a Fulbright balks or a Mansfield broods, into the
streets, to the ballot box, to the very places where men are asked to give
their lives. It is in the main a movement, furthermore, of the young,

who are in revolt in a way this nation has never before seen. It has, finally, become linked with yet another threat to the political and economic power structure—the drive of the black American for a fair share of his political and economic rights.

What follows is not in any sense intended as a judgment of the policies of the Johnson administration in Vietnam. It is an attempt to document . . . the fact that newspapers, wire services, news magazines, general magazines, radio stations and television networks have failed, in varying degrees, to report accurately the high degree of discontent with American policies in Vietnam. It would be nonsense to suggest a publishers' plot or an electronic conspiracy to deceive the American people. It is reasonable to suggest, however, that the press, as an important part of the established system, has been reluctant to report on the growth of dissent, especially when the expressions of dissent have moved beyond traditional political advocacy. Although the press constitutionally was set outside the framework of government to serve as a check on the errors and excesses of government, it nevertheless in its reporting of militant dissent has served to support policies of the governmental-industrial-military complex. . . .

So much has been written about the gathering at the Lincoln Memorial and the subsequent "confrontation" between armed troops and peace marchers at the Pentagon last October that one turns to this matter reluctantly. Nonetheless, the reporting of the events of that day stands as a revealing example of the thesis being presented here.

While the "orthodox" press passively accepted the official line of the government, or at best only mildly wondered about it, the "underground" press cited the evidence that should have been available to all citizens. . . .

Although fewer than 700 persons were arrested—less than one per cent of the demonstrators—and the vast majority behaved in an orderly, even good-humored manner, a vein of hostility to the demonstration and the demonstrators runs through most published accounts in the general-circulation press, with emphasis on violence, peculiar dress, dirtiness, marijuana and obscenity. . . .

The *Washington Post* sneered at the "shaggy doves and the sweet smell of pot," and the *National Observer* observed in its account that "the core was made up of hippies and pseudo-hippies, students and pseudo-students—a great many colorful sheep. The sheep were ready to be led. . . . Despite the gymnasium smell and the dirty hair. . . ." *Time's* accounts were filled with misleading generalities ("Within the tide of dissenters swarmed all the elements of American dissent in 1967: hard-eyed revolutionaries and skylarking hippies; ersatz motorcycle gangs and all-too-real college professors; housewives, ministers and authors;

Black Nationalists in African garb—but no real African nationalists; nonviolent pacifists and nonpacific advocates of violence. . . ."), officially sponsored innuendoes ("Dean Rusk, whose State Department intelligence apparatus had long since assessed the degree and role of Communist influence within the antiwar movement, said earlier this month that 'we haven't made public the extent of our knowledge' for fear of setting off 'a new McCarthyism.'"), and insipid insinuations (" 'You should see what we found out there,' said one worker. 'Nothing but bras and panties. You never saw so many.'"). *Newsweek* stressed Norman Mailer's "artist's freak-out," a "gaggle of hippies," the "rhetorical vitriol" at the rally and a concluding reference to an unidentified woman who "muttered as twilight descended" that she was leaving with her small son because "I guess he's seen enough democracy in action for one day."

In reporting the number of participants in the demonstration, the mass media became a partner of the government in a calculated attempt to minimize the total. The basis for the statistical hoax was that any crowd estimate must clearly delineate the time and the place. There were three major events during the day. The largest crowd gathered Saturday morning at the Lincoln Memorial, where approximately 100,000 —including those who had other plans for later in the day, curious bystanders, button salesmen, police, press, CIA and others—would be a fair estimate. . . . About 60,000 of these made the march across Arlington Memorial Bridge to the Pentagon. . . . Thousands of these persons, having made their point, were on their way back even before the end of the parade reached the Pentagon's north parking lot. At dusk, when the "confrontation" took place, more than 35,000 were on the Pentagon steps, the Mall and the grassy reaches extending to the parking lots (a figure the same as that finally issued by the Defense Department, which said it had made aerial photographs of the crowd at the Pentagon and had arrived at an estimate of 35,000 persons through military photo-inspection techniques). About 8,000 more on the parking lot did not pass beyond a point which was announced as the line to be crossed only by those who wished to push past non-violence toward civil disobedience or violent confrontation with the military. Many reports failed to distinguish between these three estimates and thereby played the Pentagon's numbers game. . . .

Thus, *Time* made much of "35,000 ranting, chanting protesters" at the Pentagon without referring to the other two-thirds of the demonstrators at the rally. . . . The *New York Times* not only accepted "a police and military consensus" that put the size of the crowd at the Lincoln Memorial at 50,000 to 55,000, but reported a "rally and march by some 50,000 persons" as if the same number had participated in both events. *U.S. News & World Report* also bought the figure of "about

55,000 persons at the Lincoln Memorial." *Newsweek* settled for a "40,000-man army of widely assorted U.S. resistance groups descending on the Capital. . . ." United Press International said "police officially estimated that between 50,000 and 55,000 persons were on hand for the rally," and accepted the word of a Pentagon spokesman who said apparently with a straight face that "between 20,000 and 25,000 protesters were at the Pentagon at the peak period of about 4 p.m. EDT." . . .

Almost as bizarre as the statistical game-playing was the photographic coverage. The mass media featured photographs of those in extremely casual or imaginative dress, and ignored the more ordinary citizens. ("Hey, take pictures of us," groups of adequately barbered and coifed, sensibly dressed marchers pleaded with photographer after photographer. "I would," a *New York Times* man responded quietly, "but they wouldn't run it.") More interesting is the absence of a photograph showing the entire crowd at the Lincoln Memorial (such as those published of the 1963 civil rights rally at the same place) or one of the parade including the beginning and some identifiable point toward the end so that an educated estimate could be made (photographers in helicopters passed over the marchers again and again), or one from the top of the Pentagon (which the Defense Department could have released to end that particular discussion). The aerial photo taken at the Pentagon, which served as the basis for military estimates, to my knowledge never has been published. And *Time,* which put a photograph of the start of the march on its cover in what it boasted was "the latest cover change we have ever made," cropped it in a curious manner. If one eliminates the bottom inconsequential 1½ inches of the Oct. 27, 1967, cover photo, an entirely different effect of a huge parade is achieved.

The "orthodox" press, with some notable exceptions, was exceedingly gentle, kind and understanding of what was probably the most blatant lie of the government—the contention of the Defense Department that soldiers at the Pentagon fired no tear gas at the demonstrators. Despite the fact that several newsmen reported that they saw tear gas canisters launched by uniformed soldiers (and I personally saw one grenade fired and experienced the effects), Pentagon spokesmen not only persisted in maintaining that the troops were innocent but that the deed was done by demonstrators. . . .

The *New York Times* gave a classic demonstration of the "orthodox" press at its best—or worst, depending on one's viewpoint. On the front page: "Several tear gas canisters exploded outside the building at various times. The Defense Department announced that the Army had not used tear gas at any time and charged that the demonstrators had." The following day it managed to return to this matter of Pentagon credibility on page 32:

There were angry charges by demonstration leaders that Defense Department officials had "lied" in denying that troops had used tear gas against the demonstrators at the Pentagon.

Last night the Department said that if tear gas had been used, it had been used by the demonstrators against the troops.

There was no question that tear gas had been used. Fumes lingered on the damp air last night for hours. Troops, demonstrators and newsmen far from the immediate scene sneezed and suffered runny noses and itching eyes until after 10 p.m.

And scores of participants and some newsmen said today that they had observed soldiers using tear gas against the demonstrators. . . .

In this fashion is the matter of truth and falsehood allowed to remain moot.

Mention also should be made of the case of the alleged defectors at the Pentagon. The "underground" press repeatedly has insisted that some soldiers—the number cited ranges from one to four—refused to follow orders and were placed under arrest. The important point is not that one or two or three or four soldiers could not bring themselves to carry out their duties at the Pentagon—there is little significance in that. It is not even a critical example of the government not telling the truth, even when the truth wouldn't really hurt. What is important, and alarming, is that the question is not even raised in the "orthodox" press. The dangers cannot be exaggerated, or the responsibilities of the press in this area minimized. . . .

Perhaps it is too much to expect, as the hostile critics of the press have contended through the years, that a press with an undeniable stake in the economic and political system would report fairly on those who are fundamentally dissatisfied with the status quo. . . .

17 Coverage of War and National Security

For more than a year, James Reston of the **New York Times** knew that the United States was flying high-altitude spy planes (U-2s) over the Soviet Union. His paper did not report the fact. Then, in 1960, a U-2 was shot down and its pilot captured. President Eisenhower denied everything. The **Times,** which knew the denials were lies, printed them without comment. Only after the President finally admitted the truth did the **Times** finally publish the truth.

Reston believes this was a correct judgment. "In this time of half-war and half-peace," he says, "that old principle of publish-and-be-damned, while very romantic, bold and hairy, can often damage the national interest."

No doubt there are times when American military adventures should not be reported by the mass media. Equally clearly, there are times when it is vitally important that those adventures be reported. The problem is telling one from the other.

When in doubt, the media typically kill the story. With the benefit of hindsight, we can find hundreds of articles that should have been published and were not. There are many fewer cases of published articles that did serious damage to national security.

American journalists have traditionally drawn a hard-and-fast line between wartime (when censorship is accepted without question) and peacetime (when it is not). This longstanding distinction is now permanently muddled. The undeclared conflict in Southeast Asia is a war. The ongoing struggle against the "Communist menace" is a war. The occasional "peace-keeping action" in Latin America or the Middle East is a war. The stockpiling of missiles and atomic bombs is a war. In these terms, the United States has been constantly at war since the 1940s and will remain at war for the foreseeable future. Does this mean that wartime standards of self-censorship should remain in force? Perhaps so.

Self-censorship isn't the whole problem, of course. The question of whether to publish or not to publish is not always left up to the media themselves. Sometimes the government has an opinion too.

During a declared war, government censorship is a straightforward affair. The media are simply told what they can print and what they cannot; correspondents are told what they can write and what they cannot. The forbidden list may include anything from a curseword to a weather report, from news of troop movements to news of troop morale —anything that might give aid and comfort to the enemy.

This sort of thing is illegal in a cold war or an undeclared war. So instead of censoring the news, the government lies about it. As one assistant secretary of defense put it in the 1960s: "I think the inherent right of the government to lie—to lie to save itself when faced with nuclear disaster—is basic, **basic.**" He might have added (but did not) that the government is equally tempted to lie when faced with loss of national prestige or the threat of a protest movement back home.

The story of the war in Vietnam, for example, is the story of an ever widening government "credibility gap." First we claimed there was no war; then we claimed we had it won; then we claimed it was not going to get bigger; then we claimed we had it won again. For nearly a decade the media meekly went along. Correspondents who told the unpleasant truth were harassed by the military or replaced by their editors. Most correspondents were content to serve as mailmen instead of newsmen, faithfully delivering to their readers the claims of U.S. military and diplomatic sources.

The successful Tet offensive of late 1967 finally convinced the media that the official truth was not the whole truth. From then on, coverage of the war grew more and more aggressive and critical. Still, the My Lai atrocity story of 1969 was revealed by a free-lance writer in Washington, not the Saigon press corps. And a six-day news embargo during the 1971 invasion of Laos was respected and obeyed by all the mass media in America.

Vietnam was television's war. It is hard to say what effect TV has had on the war. On the one hand, it made public the horrors of war;

on the other hand, it turned those horrors into exciting adventure stories. Even after the Tet offensive, television confined itself largely to a sanitized, though colorful, picture of the daily battlefield. Complex issues were ignored or oversimplified; emotional responses were suppressed.

But there are exceptions. In the face of all kinds of pressures and problems, television occasionally comes up with a sensitive piece of interpretive war journalism. The selection that follows offers one example.

MICHAEL J. ARLEN

Morley Safer's Vietnam

. . . This is probably as good a time as any to say that although television news is often maddeningly bad (inept, bland, secondhand, simplistic—a dozen cautions rolled into one), it can at times be very good indeed, as was a sixty-minute report called "Morley Safer's Vietnam," which CBS News presented last week. Safer's hour struck me, quite simply, as one of the best pieces of journalism to come out of the Vietnam war in any medium, and a large measure of its success seemed to be due to the fact that Safer (who has been a CBS correspondent in Vietnam for the past few years) was permitted to put the film together in his own way, with his own explicit point of view, with his own apparently strong sense of irony (you certainly don't see much of that on network news), and to be as personal as he wanted to be. The key word is "personal." There just hasn't been much personal reporting out of Vietnam by the networks (or the newspapers or the big magazines); it's as if it were all too large and important for one man to hoist aloft with an individual point of view—which is a pity, since although there are plenty of situations in which so-called factual, objective reporting makes sense, gives you something useful, there are a lot of other situations in which

From *Living-Room War* by Michael J. Arlen (New York: The Viking Press, Inc., 1969), pp. 61–65. Copyright © 1967 by Michael J. Arlen. All rights reserved. Originally appeared in *The New Yorker*. Reprinted by permission of the Viking Press, Inc.

no useful facts are given, or in which many of the facts are somehow irrelevant (U.S. FORCES KILL 55 VIETCONG IN RAID), answering little and leaving the important questions (and answers) out there hidden in the fog.   What Safer did was to grab off small handfuls of Vietnam—the people, the soldiers, the countryside, the dead, the living—and say, "This is who *I* am, this is how it looks and feels to *me*," and the result was as moving and as tough and as sensitive and as deeply felt a commentary on the war as I've run into.

It's nearly impossible, I know, to describe something like Safer's program in print with any success, especially since so much of this particular film's impact was in the sound of the dialogue and in the editing and cutting.   For example, there was a sequence beginning with General Westmoreland visiting some troops in the field—the General, tall, strange, remote, looking down upon some young kid standing at attention out there in a Vietnamese clearing, his young face half hidden by a helmet liner, and asking him the kind of questions that, in other times and places, are supposed to connect people but that in this time and place seem only to confirm an unbelievable, nonhuman apartness:

> WESTMORELAND: How's your morale?
> GI: Pretty good, sir.
> WESTMORELAND: How's your food?
> GI: Real good, sir.
> WESTMORELAND: Son, what state are you from?
> GI: Texas, sir.
> WESTMORELAND: What part?
> GI: Southwest. Shullerville . . .
> WESTMORELAND: How old are you, son?
> GI: Twenty years old, sir.
> WESTMORELAND: Twenty years.   Where did you get your basic training?
> GI: Fort Polk, Louisiana, sir.

It was absolutely dreamlike, and could have been out of an old movie. (Has there ever been a general since Alexander the Great who didn't stand sternly before his young soldiers, his own eyes staring through their heads and out beyond to India or Hanoi, and ask them, in flat, abstracted tones, where they took their basic training?) Safer then cut to another GI, a nice-looking young kid standing silhouetted against a line of trees and speaking in an easy-going, modest voice:

> GI: I don't like my job.
> SAFER: How's that?
> GI: I'd rather be back home.
> SAFER: What don't you like about it?

GI: Just—I don't like riding the people's gardens down. And just, I'd rather be back home.

Then back to Westmoreland, interviewing an officer whose company has just been under fire:

WESTMORELAND: Was he killed?
OFFICER: Yes, sir, he was literally blown apart.

Then back to Safer, talking to another GI:

SAFER: How about the brass?
GI: They're not bad over here. . . . They don't worry you.
SAFER: Just that Army life doesn't agree with you?
GI: No, I'd rather be a civilian. I'm a civilian at heart.

Then a final glimpse of Westmoreland, giving a speech to the men he's been visiting:

It's a matter of great pride to me to see the high morale that has obtained with the troops—well, for the last year and a half, when we've had a substantial number of troops here. I attribute this to many things. First, they believe that they are performing an important mission. They take pride in doing a good job. They find this a very exciting experience. The food is good. The mail service is excellent, although from time to time there are delays—but these are exceptional.

I guess it's fair to say that Morley Safer isn't exactly happy about the Vietnam war, and since I'm not, either (as who is?), I may be guilty of admiring my own prejudices in what he showed us. But what I like to think I admire a whole lot more is his ability (and, for that matter, CBS's willingness) to risk an explicitly personal statement, and to bring a strong sense of irony to bear upon the war—although I can't see how it's really possible anywhere, any time, to report a war without irony. There was a whole lot of plain feeling, too, for the rigors of combat, for the strange languid rhythms of Army life, the softball playing, the waiting, the sleeping, the waiting, the writing letters home (only now they record them on tape), and especially for the particular time and place, our Army *there* and what *there* is—the people, the countryside, Saigon, the tanks, the peasants, the tanks *and* peasants. And a lot of toughness. I'm thinking, for example, of a scene outside an Army hospital in which a bunch of wounded men were watching a girl—as it happened, Nancy Sinatra—a real miniskirted babe in a Hollywood cowboy outfit and blue suède boots, prancing about on the grass and belting out a rock number, "These Boots Are Made for Walking," and, of course (or not of course), dozens of the men watching her, from beds or from wheelchairs, had bandages around their legs, or no legs, or no feet. This is one of the more familiar ironies of war (I guess), but it was damned real and brutal, with the camera cutting back and forth between Nancy Sinatra, in her blue boots, and all those wounded men, who were obviously enjoying themselves—taking pictures of Nancy Sinatra with their cameras. Nancy Sinatra looked like such a doll. The sun was shining. The band was loud. The song was great.

There were other strong moments. A scene of Madame Ky, along with other highborn or at least high-placed Vietnamese ladies and remnants of the French colony (all beautifully gussied up in 1938 Deauville dresses), attending the annual garden show in Saigon. A scene in which a burly Negro soldier was washing the head of a litle Vietnamese kid and muttering gruffly about the bad "hygiene habits" of the South Vietnamese. A remarkable dialogue in a service club, where Safer was interviewing the crew of an attack helicopter recently returned from a mission, the men smiling, relaxed, milling around with their beer cans—all nice boys. Safer asked them, "How do you feel when you make a kill like that?"

PILOT: I feel sort of detached from the whole thing. It's not personal. . . .

CAPTAIN: I feel real good when we do it. It's kind of a feeling of accomplishment. It's the only way you're going to win, I guess, is to kill 'em.

THIRD PILOT: I just feel like it's just another target. You know, like in the States you shot at dummies, over here you shoot at Vietnamese. Vietnamese Cong.

ANOTHER PILOT'S VOICE (*interrupting*): Cong. You shoot at Cong. You don't shoot at Vietnamese.

THIRD PILOT (*laughing*): All right. You shoot at Cong. Anyway, when you come out on the run and then you see them, and they come into your sights, it's just like a wooden dummy or something there, you just thumb off a couple pair of rockets. Like they weren't people at all.

Or when Safer was interviewing a young soldier, one of those fair-haired, blue-eyed soldiers with seemingly untouched farmboy faces, and was asking him what he felt about the war. The boy started out with what one imagines is the usual sort of mechanical response—"I'd be lying if I said I was glad to be here, but since I am here I'm glad to be doing what I'm doing"—and then, in one of those sudden moments when everything comes alive in a gesture, a look in the eye, he glanced around him, his face for one instant full of surprised affection. "The country's so *beautiful*, fertile, and everything . . ." he said.

It was an excellent film. The cameraman who shot much of it, by the way, was Ha Thuc Can, a Vietnamese.

18   Coverage of Race

The media discovered race in 1954.   Prior to that time the white press totally ignored the black community; criminals, athletes, and comic movie menials were the only black faces to be found in the media.   An entirely separate system of black newspapers had developed to meet the needs that the white media were not meeting.   It helped blacks communicate with each other, but of course it provided no communication at all between the two races.

Then, in 1954, the Supreme Court announced its school-desegregation decision and the modern civil-rights movement was born.   As far as the white media were concerned, it was a virgin birth—the movement came out of nowhere, with no hint of longstanding grievances.   Reporters on the so-called "seg beat" were sent south for months at a time, to tell the story of blacks valiantly struggling for their freedom from southern oppressors.   The reporters were horrified by what they saw, and their sense of outrage permeated their stories.

Civil-rights reporters invaded Mississippi and Alabama by the hundreds, but very few bothered to visit the northern ghettos in their own backyard.   These local sores were permitted to fester, unattended, until the Watts riot of 1965.   Then, suddenly, the media discovered all over again that black people were big news.

The media have done a generally adequate job of covering the facts of racial unrest.   But the grievances and life-styles behind that unrest are another story—a story that the media have left untold or badly told for generations.   The everyday life of the ghetto—weddings and dances, drugs and tenements, births and deaths—seldom makes the pages of the white press.   And when it does, it is often slanted in a way that opens the media to the charge of racism, at least unconscious racism.   Not too long ago, the **New York Times** ran an article on President Johnson's farewell to a group of high-ranking black government officials.   It carefully referred to "the well-dressed Negro officials and their wives."   Would the **Times** have bothered to note that about a white group?

One reason why the media have failed to tell the black story properly is that they have lacked black reporters to help them tell it.   Only in the last few years have the media seriously recruited black journalists (on at least a token basis)—and they still do very little to train promising black candidates.

When a black reporter is hired, should he be assigned to the ghetto or should he be given a full range of stories?   There are good arguments both ways.   But one thing is certain: Most white reporters are clearly unable or unwilling to do a good job of ghetto coverage.   In the selection that follows, the white civil-rights reporter for the **Newark** (N.J.) **News** describes his work.   His good intentions are obvious.   But his glowing account was published only months before the disastrous Newark riots of 1967.

REPORTING ON RACE

By DOUGLAS ELDRIDGE

In the last few years the civil rights movement has produced thousands of new jobs across the country.

In a sense, one of those new jobs is mine.

I have been the civil rights reporter for the *Newark News* since 1963, when race relations suddenly became a national preoccupation.

This unusual new job has been big, busy and—to a reporter who felt at loose ends on general assignment—thoroughly engrossing.

My paper is the largest in New Jersey.   Its home town has the highest percentage of Negro population of any major city in the North.   An estimated 50 percent of Newark's 400,000 residents are nonwhite —so we don't have to look far for all the civil rights stories any paper could possibly cover.

From *Editor & Publisher*, 100, no. 8 (February 25, 1967), 13, 52.   Reprinted by permission.

In the last four years this beat has taken many forms: Listening to street-corner firebrands, discussing personnel techniques with businessmen, watching marchers outside schools and stores, poring over antipoverty plans and budgets, attending meetings at city hall or in church basements, compiling files on scores of subjects, trailing political campaign motorcades, and interviewing everyone—high or low—who might shed light on community problems.

This beat has ranged from national events, like the 1963 March on Washington, to cases with only personal significance —like the welfare recipient whose check is late this month.

Coverage of Newark's large and growing Negro community is nothing new for the News. Our files contain hundreds of clippings on racial controversies and social ills in bygone decades. The paper has had at least one Negro reporter most of the time since the early 1950s, and now has four.

But it was not until 1963 that the editors found it necessary to assign someone to specific and continual coverage of civil rights. And then my beat —much like the civil rights movement—began out of town, and developed almost by chance.

Early in 1963 some Negro leaders in Newark began a drive for a civilian police review board. Our city editor, Harry Anderson, sent me to Philadelphia to study that city's review board. Afterward, I covered the issue in Newark—

rallies, forums and hearings— and in the process, I came to know most civil rights groups and leaders in the city.

After their review board campaign failed, the Newark rights groups in the summer of 1963 went after the building trades unions. Since I already knew the Negro leaders involved, I was sent to cover parts of that battle, too. And after the March on Washington in August, 1963, I was assigned to cover civil rights day by day.

In 1964 and 1965 the beat evolved, and extended inevitably, to anti-poverty and job training programs, public welfare and general social issues. By last year, as commotion o v e r discrimination waned in Newark, we were devoting more time and space to poverty than to civil rights stories.

But even today my beat— like civil rights and poverty— has no clear or rigid boundaries. Partly this reflects the free hand I am given by my editors.

As an old college newspaper rebel, I may view this freedom with some skepticism. But it is there, all the same. I am encouraged to cover nearly everything I want to cover, and my stories are rarely changed for any reason but length. . . .

A friend once called my job "the anti–city hall beat." But it goes beyond that. It has taken me to meetings and marches in Washington and Trenton—as well as at the city welfare office just across the street.

It has taken me to sessions of every kind of group, including political, neighborhood and Negro organizations that have little direct involvement in civil rights.

My first order of business has been the straight news coverage of all the civil rights and anti-poverty activity of recent years—all the angry and complex demonstrations and negotiations about housing, employment, schools and police, as well as rallies, dinners, seminars, hearings and press conferences.

But daily coverage was only the beginning. There have also been series (e.g., public welfare, the war on poverty); surveys of local opinion (on "black power," civil rights laws, prospects for summer peace); historical studies (the Negro in Newark, Emancipation in New Jersey); personality pieces (a new anti-poverty official, a retiring CORE leader); analyses (an NAACP election battle, a federal fund cutback), and periodic reports on all kinds of programs and organizations, from construction unions to the Muslims.

In many cases we have little choice of what to cover. Events happen in civil rights as in other fields, and we report on them.

But sometimes we get the chance—and the time—to choose. Then we try to delve into long-term developments that may be less dramatic but more important than the promoters and protestors clamoring for front-page attention.

We have given extensive coverage, including a five-part series, to efforts by local businessmen and civil rights leaders to resolve their differences and mount a joint assault on discrimination and unemployment. We have emphasized much of the "good" but often overlooked news on integration—such as the record numbers of job placements by the local Urban League. And we make periodic checks on poverty and training projects to see how they measure up to advance ballyhoo.

The goal is always to be full and fair, but with some sensitivity and self-restraint. We do not overlook any group, however disreputable or dangerous it may seem; but we do not think the wildest accusation or direct threat warrants the biggest headline.

This civil-rights beat poses many pitfalls for any reporter. I tackled it after four years on a college daily and six years in general assignment and police reporting. But I had no particular preparation for my current job, and little contact with the Negro community. So I've had to develop various techniques to overcome—or at least cover—my early handicaps in this field. . . .

I attend meetings of as many groups as possible, even when agendas are barren. I visit offices and project sites, and tour the city's slums whenever I can. I read Negro magazines and papers, and reports of many organizations. I file all material I can find on civil rights and poverty—a task that is mostly drudgery, but produces invaluable background.

Most of all, I try to make

and keep contacts. This is done on any beat, of course, but here there may be some added barriers—race, culture and emotion—between the reporter and his possible sources.

My favorite technique is just talk—with as many people on as many subjects in as casual an atmosphere as climate. I often linger after a meeting—one luxury of working on an evening paper—to renew acquaintances. I often interview more people than I really need for a particular story—just so no possible base is untouched, or angle unnoticed.

A sidewalk chat often yields tips and ideas. A routine phone check on some information often becomes a quick survey of the local scene. (And I have found civil rights is one beat where the telephone is sometimes more effective than face-to-face contact, because it removes the visibility of race.)

. . .

Sometimes a casual discussion really pays off. At a sidewalk barbecue last summer a civil rights worker mentioned to me that the police seemed friendlier than in the past. His one remark led to two dozen interviews, and a three-part series on improving relations between police and the nonwhite public.

In all conversations I try to follow one basic rule: Be as polite and pleasant as possible. I'm tempted often to be argumentative rather than agreeable, especially when the press is being raked over the coals. But then I remember my job is not to win debates but to get information—and I have to roll with the punches.

I find that an easy-going,

low-key approach gets the best response. Hard-nosed interviewing may work with public officials. But it only backfires with people who have a deep-rooted suspicion of newspapers.

The biggest problem on my beat—and I suspect it's greater there than on other beats—is the gulf of understanding between the reporter and the people making the news.

I recall one news story in which a young Negro leader was mistakenly identified. I knew the error was simple sloppiness—but the young man bitterly insisted it was part of a plot by the press to discredit the civil rights movement.

Many Negroes have had little direct contact with the press. Many see it as part of "the power structure"—a downtown institution that has little to do with everyday life in the ghetto. The one complaint I hear most often is that the press notices the Negro community only when it misbehaves.

On the other hand, most reporters—including me—have had little regular exposure to slum life. We have perhaps assumed that what goes on there isn't news—that the people who make news must live elsewhere.

To be sure, civil rights has its celebrities. I have interviewed Dr. Martin Luther King at the airport, accompanied Bayard Rustin on a tour of a decaying neighborhood, listened to Roy Wilkins at banquets—and Stokely Carmichael in the streets.

But most of the time I deal with people whose names do

not usually make news. They are the strangers, the outsiders, the losers in our society—and I may look in vain for ordinary credentials or clearcut motives. But what these people think and do is having a profound impact on our cities—and it must be reported.

Bridging the gap poses a special challenge for a white reporter. It is impossible to cover race relations without being reminded of your own race—sometimes painfully.

Some months ago I went to visit a slum tenement. As I climbed the unswept stairs, some Negro youngsters playing on the landing called to me: "Hey, mister, are you the insurance collector?" I told them I wasn't, and continued my climb.

The people I wanted to see weren't in, and I started back down the stairs. At the landing, one little boy taunted me: "Ha-ha, you didn't get anything, did you?"

It was a sharp reminder that I—just because I was white—was automatically seen as an exploiter in the ghetto, even by children. And the little boy couldn't help rejoicing that I left empty-handed.

The fact that I am white has been an occasional handicap. I can hardly pay an inconspicuous visit to a Negro church or tavern, and I've been mistaken for a detective or a public official. Some Negroes have made it clear they don't like white people looking in on their activities—particularly the power struggles in their own organizations—and they don't think any white reporter can understand their problems.

There is some validity in this feeling. But I am still glad my paper usually assigns reporters without regard for race.

Civil rights, after all, does involve more than one race, and it must be reported and analyzed for whites as well as Negroes. I already know how whites may think and feel, and it is my job to try to find out—on behalf of all my readers—how Negroes may think and feel.

Moreover, I have found that repeated appearance in the Negro community of a white reporter, willing to listen and to learn, can take some of the edge off hostility toward the press.

This brings up what may be the biggest challenge of all—trying to be accurate and impartial in writing about a subject that is elusive and volatile, surrounded by intangibles and imponderables, and laden with emotion for almost every reader. One story on a racial issue may draw more intense reaction than a hundred pieces on some other topic. . . .

I have to be on guard against a problem that can arise on any beat—one-sidedness—and has extra implications here. Sometimes it isn't easy to assert your independence as a reporter—as when a zealous woman grabs your arm and starts swaying during the singing of "We Shall Overcome" at a street rally. . . .

I was reminded of the danger of over-identification with

my subject a few years ago. A prominent Negro who had never met me invited me to his office to discuss a job possibility—and then discovered to his dismay that I was white.

"I've been reading all your articles," he said, "and I just assumed you were a Negro." I told him I didn't know quite what to make of that remark— (I still don't)—and left as gracefully as possible.

There are other difficulties, too, in covering a subject that is often kept behind the scenes —either because the participants are scared of the press, or don't know how to deal with it. Public relations, I have found, is an almost unknown art among many of the groups I cover. . . .

But there are plenty of satisfactions, too. There was my discovery, for one, that the press can play a major role in providing communication and clearing up misunderstanding among divergent forces in a city. I have found that the local press is the only medium that can reach nearly every social and economic level in a community. (This is particularly the case in Newark, which has no network radio or television outlets, and is generally ignored by the electronic media in nearby New York.)

I've also found that newspaper coverage is an important route to recognition for many groups. Just by doing its job and covering all parts of a city, a paper like the *Newark News* can help counteract feelings of isolation or neglect among those who are black or poor, or both. I do not want to make claims, but I wonder if newspaper coverage is one of the many reasons Newark has somehow avoided the racial explosions that beset many other cities the last three years.

When I look at the long and growing list of stories I ought to do, I'm more convinced than ever that civil rights and poverty are a legitimate beat, and need the most careful and consistent coverage.

A couple of summers ago, after the eruption in Watts, I dug out an old air raid helmet from a storeroom at the *News*. But fortunately Newark was spared and I never had to use the hat. It finally disappeared last year.

I haven't even looked for another helmet. Instead, I'm hoping more than ever that I can just keep doing my job— and that I will continue to need a level head more than a covered one.

19   Coverage
of Specialized News

Certain favored categories of news are not required to compete with political stories and the like for time, space, and manpower.   Instead, they are organized into their own special sections of a newspaper, magazine, or broadcast news program.   Often these special sections are very popular—but the news they offer is usually substandard.

Consider, for example, the business section of your local newspaper, which probably runs three or four pages a day—more space than is allotted even to political news.   Why all this special attention?   Business news is important, of course, but it is also cheap and easy to gather.   The biggest chunk of the business section consists of the stock tables.   These come direct from AP or UPI by high-speed wire, ready to be inserted into the paper.   No editing is required, and a computer can do the typesetting.   National business and economic stories also come via wire.   As for local business and financial news, that comes in "over the transom"— press releases by the bushel from every company in town.   A business reporter can work for years without ever leaving his desk.   Some do. Many more leave their desks mainly to attend lavish press luncheons, boozy retirement banquets, and free junkets to new factories in exotic places.

Good business reporting, of course, is by no means cheap or easy.

It takes a lot of digging to get the truth from corporate public-relations types. And it takes a lot of training to know the truth when you find it. And it takes a lot of writing skill to translate the truth into language a layman can understand. But most business reporters seldom bother to try. They just print the press releases and leave it at that.

Other specialized departments are equally irresponsible. For example:

- The travel pages seldom say anything bad about any vacation spot —unless it drops its ads.
- The religion page prefers puffery for local churches to controversial religious reporting.
- The real-estate section ignores crucial "quality of life" questions and caters to advertisers instead.
- The sports section is written by inveterate fans who call themselves newsmen; no game is ever dull.
- The women's department devotes itself almost exclusively to recipies, beauty hints, and other consumer-oriented topics.
- The entertainment pages are loaded with light features on sexy stars and contain very little else.

These specialized stories are decidedly substandard—but at least they get into the paper. Not even that can be said for specialized news that has no department of its own. A science story, for example, must compete for space on the general news pages. Solid science, written by trained science writers, is very unlikely to win in such a competition. What sort of science does win? Sensational headlines—the first man on the moon. Human-interest features—handsome Dr. Christiaan Barnard and his transplants. Humor—the discovery of the sex-lure chemical by which the female cockroach calls her boyfriend to a date. And that's about all.

In areas like science, medicine, education, and labor, only the most sensational and the most amusing stories are likely to reach the public. This is equally true in the field of foreign affairs—perhaps the most important specialized topic of all.

War zones aside, there are fewer than 500 full-time American newsmen abroad. That does not seem like much to cover an entire world, especially since the bulk of the reporters are concentrated in Europe. But remember, foreign correspondents are expensive. Moreover, foreign news is dull. The average American adult reads only twelve column inches of foreign news a day, spending roughly two minutes and twenty seconds on the job. Given this meager demand, 500 overseas correspondents begin to sound pretty generous.

Nearly all the foreign news that reaches the American public falls into one of three categories: (1) Political news from official government sources; (2) Sensational news of earthquakes, riots, strikes, and assassinations; and (3) Colorful news with a strong, American human-interest angle ("Hot Dogs Big Hit in Iran"). Backgrounding is nonexistent. "Do you want to read about the Sudan when nothing 'big' is happening there?" asks one reporter. "Well, good luck if you do." The point, of course, is that very few Americans **do** want to read such a story.

The selection that follows describes the activities of the wire services in Latin America.

PETER BARNES

The Wire Services in Latin America

For some time now, Latin America has been at a turning point in its history, a turning point which has taken centuries to arrive at and may take decades more to navigate. . . .

This turning point was reached in Latin America well before Fidel Castro made the United States somewhat vaguely, and uneasily, aware of it. But Latin America, one of the three major areas that constitute the western family of nations, was the forgotten member of that family—not only in our press, but in our educational system, in tourism, in the disposal of economic aid and in policy making priorities. . . .

In maintaining our democracy on an even keel with reality, the press has one of its prime responsibilities. There can be no doubt that the press possesses the power to build up images and stereotypes, particularly about things distant from the reader. Two great wire services span the U.S., and between them provide Americans with the lion's share of their daily information about Latin America. The Associated Press and UPI both feed upwards of 1,100 newspapers. The average reader has little other information with which to judge the veracity of the wire services, or question their emphases.

Reprinted from *Nieman Reports*, March, 1964, by permission, Society of Nieman Fellows.

The questions that must be asked, then, are several. Do the news agencies keep the U.S. adequately and acurately supplied with hard news from Latin America? Do they keep us adequately and accurately provided with interpretive news from that changing area? Is the overall image created of Latin America by both kinds of news stories a just one, or is it, as most Latins who visit the U.S. and read our press claim, a distorted, "underdeveloped" image? . . .

The American news agency activities in Latin America have their origin in the 1893 agreement between the then Big Four in news distribution, Reuters, AP, Havas and Wolff. Under the cartel arrangement, AP was given the rights to the U.S., and later to Mexico and Central America. Reuters distributed AP's American news abroad . . . and handled the British Empire and the Far East. South America was ceded to Havas.

Then, in June 1907, what was later to burgeon into United Press International began as an agglomeration of correspondents incorporated into a single profit-seeking agency by Edward Wyliss Scripps. Unfettered by the agreements which bound AP, a cooperative news-gathering service, UP was eager to open up new markets.

The opportunity came in 1914 after AP's general manager, Melville A. Stone, loyal to his international commitments, discarded a plea from publisher Jorge Mitre of *La Nación* (Buenos Aires) to supply it with balanced World War coverage. Havas was giving neutral South America only the French side of the war.

UP, which next received Mitre's offer, snapped it up avidly. Roy Howard, news manager of UP, sent Charles P. Stewart down to Buenos Aires as the first U.S. bureau chief in Latin America. Then in 1916, Howard himself went down to South America, firmed up Mitre, and acquired several other clients for the UP. . . .

Today, after an aggressive, if belated expansion drive during the past few years, AP, with 306 Latin American subscribers, still trails UPI, with 650, and Agence France Presse, the government-supported successor to Havas. . . .

These various and mostly conservative clients provide the wire services with enough revenues to maintain a staff of correspondents in Latin America who, in turn, are the gatherers of news for the U.S. reader. The situation is such, however, that the Latin American countries are covered by agencies that are foreign to them, in the same way that Reuters was foreign to the U.S.; and that the two American agencies which report Latin America for the U.S. have their own economic interests to defend. The influence of the agencies' clients will be mentioned later.

In staffing and organization, the AP and UPI are essentially similar in Latin America. Both fan out their communications networks from New York by way of radio, commercial and leased cable, telephone, and telex. Both maintain bureaus (two or more newsmen) in the major cities of the major countries, and stringers in the rest of the countries and smaller cities.

In all, UPI claims to have 124 full-time newsmen on its staff in Latin America (which is either an exaggeration or a gross stretching of terms), and AP more realistically says it has 43. Whatever the exact totals, UPI does have more than AP.

Approximately 70% of news agency staffers in Latin America are nationals, with UPI, because of its larger Latin American clientele, having a slightly higher proportion than AP. If any generalization can be made about these non-American staffers, it would be that the majority of them are underpaid, under-motivated, and under-trained, and that many of them have vested reasons—political, family, or other—for not giving an objective treatment of the news. The average salary for a fairly well remunerated local stringer in Latin America is around $85 a month—and their gripe is that Americans get more.

Of the news that is sent to New York by the wire service correspondents about 20%, according to their own estimates (it was less before Castro), gets through the foreign news desks and on to the domestic wires. A smaller part moves on to the world desk and off to London. And the bulk returns to Latin America where, along with the rest of the news agencies' Latin American services, the interested countries or regions pick it up.

The crux of the matter, however, is not really how much news gets sent (it is far more than is used by local American telegraph editors anyway) but what kind. Against those who claim that the agencies' coverage of Latin American news is too sensationalistic, too over-simplified, or too obsessed with salable punchlines, the agencies argue that you can only write news of unfamiliar lands by making it understandable in familiar terms. Were Latin American coverage not like this, few Americans would read news of that area at all. Better to have the public superficially informed than to have them ignorant of Latin American affairs altogether, runs the argument. . . .

A bi-lingual member of the UPI Caracas bureau explained: "I write the English material for the U.S. and Europe. This includes news with an international implication, such as the communist terrorism here, especially when the attacks are against U.S. companies. (It doesn't matter so much if the national Architecture School here is bombed.) It also includes crashes, disasters, baseball scores, and anything spectacular, such as the theft of pictures from the national art gallery. We used to do stories on the activities of the Cuban exiles in Venezuela, but people got tired of that. And we also do bits in English on odd things of international interest: Angel waterfall, the highest in the world, and the fact that you can ski in Venezuela just one hour from the tropical sea coast.

"On politics, the only things we send to the U.S. deal with Fidel Castro, Betancourt's fight against communist subversion, and the Alliance for Progress, though that's a pretty nebulous thing. All the rest goes in Spanish for Latin American consumption, or it just doesn't get reported. We write up in Spanish a great deal more about national politics because the Latin American nations have similar problems and customs, and can more readily understand it.". . .

For the homeside view of the selection process, a recent study of Latin American coverage made by the Fund for the Republic is useful. This study, it should be said, has been severely criticized on methodological grounds by news agency executives and even by some newsmen participating in it. Nevertheless, taking its figures with allowance for this, the part of the study that tabulates the number of wire service items on U.S. trunk wires is still significant.

In the one-month period of February, 1962, according to the study, four items about Colombia passed the AP foreign news desk and appeared on the A wire. A comparable figure held for UPI. Other countries, with the exception of Cuba, got similar exposure to local telegraph editors' snippers. In short, Hal Hendrix of the Scripps-Howard newspapers, who worked on this part of the study, was led to conclude: "It seems from the month's sampling that the long-standing attitude of the Latin American about the presentation of news of his problems and of his nation in the U.S. still holds true—revolutions, earthquakes and other catastrophes make news in the U.S. press." For our purposes, it serves to underline where the brunt of Latin American news, and particularly the substantive news, gets selected out: not so much down on the scene, as in New York.

Other factors, besides hard news selection, contribute to the formation of an overall image of Latin America. The most important of these is style.

American news agency style, increasingly setting the pace for journalism throughout the world, is crisp, curt, and condensed. A passion for numbers adds an aura of factuality that is misleading. The pyramid structure, convenient for harried telegraph editors, arranges facts and meaning according to a journalistic scale of news value.

This agency style has many advantages, the foremost being the time and organization of thought it saves the reader. But it also lends itself in several places to distortions. First, the lead and pyramid form inherently blows up a single aspect at the expense of all others in the reader's mind. And since the criteria for lead selection on Latin American copy heavily favors deaths and crises—as does the criteria for news selection—these aspects again dominate the total image, or are not sufficiently counter-balanced by others. On riot or terrorist stories, the number of dead and the value of damages always precedes all other information. The political causes, pre-conditions, and motives, which all such events have and which should be of greater, more lasting importance than the number of deaths, are relegated to the tail ends of these stories, if they are treated at all.

Secondly, the hard-hitting American style calls for liberal use of descriptive nouns and verbs. . . . Wire service dispatches have Castro "bellowing" to "mobs," Che Guevara spouting forth "harangues" at international conferences, and health campaigns in Cuba being labeled as "propaganda drives." In a dispatch from Chile, people were described as having been "lured" into voting for the left-wing FRAP. More palatable causes to the U.S., needless to say, get the opposite treatment.

Another predilection of the economy-minded U.S. style is the "nutshell epithet" to convey briefly the position of parties and men. While it is perfectly possible for such epithets to be without connotations of value judgment, all too many of them as used by the agencies are not as unintended to prejudice as they might be. Here are some actual examples of these ready-made labels which agencies insert almost automatically when mention of their wearer is made:

". . . Romulo Betancourt, first freely elected President of Venezuela to serve out his full term in office . . ."

". . . Leonel Brizola, fiery leftist brother-in-law of President Goulart . . ."

". . . the FRAP (Chilean Popular Front), a Communist-led five-party alliance pledged to make this Latin American country a Red-controlled state . . ."

". . . Peron, former dictator of Argentina . . ."

". . . Alfonso Lopez Michelson (moderate Colombian progressive), whose party is rife with supporters of Fidel Castro . . ."

And so on. The upshot of this agency name-tagging, which fortunately other news sources such as the New York *Times* manage to avoid, is the creation of a virtual pantheon of heroes and bogey men in the world of U.S. press imagery. . . . There is nothing wrong with having preferences and dislikes, but not to the extreme where we know little in the U.S. about the legitimate criticisms raised in their own countries against the heroes, and even less about the legitimate accomplishments of the bogey men. . . .

It must be recognized in any discussion of this subject that the agencies are facing an essentially thankless task in bringing Latin American news to the U.S. They are trying to inform a reading public about a land which it has never studied in its high school or college history classes, never fought in as a GI, hardly ever visited as a tourist, and with which it rarely has ethnic or ancestral ties. Yet, despite many shortcomings, the agencies have made considerable strides since the advent of Fidel Castro. . . .

In the last analysis, the problem of wire service coverage of Latin America boils down to the fact that the U.S., despite Fidel Castro, still is not sufficiently aware of or interested in the 20 republics to the south. An informal poll of managing editors of 25 leading newspapers across the country, taken by this writer, showed that except for special cases on the southern border of our nation, the majority frankly felt that there just wasn't much interest in their community for Latin America. A typical reply was one such as this:

> With all due respect for human interests, I think that, though there are some people in any community who have some interest in Latin American affairs, this number is nowhere near the number interested in a local murder. Readers are, and I suppose always will be, interested in events as they can see they are affected by them. The relevancy of most Latin American news is lost on them.

Yet, the press is a major factor in this general inability to see the relevance of Latin America, and the wire services, as main purveyors of news to the nation, must bear a substantial brunt of the burden of educating it. . . .

Epilogue

All the selections in this book deal with specific situations and problems. Nearly all are critical of the mass media. The editors believe these criticisms are valid—that is why the selections were chosen.

Nonetheless, it is important to preserve a sense of perspective. With all their flaws, the American media are probably both the most independent and the most responsible media in the world. The best of modern American journalism is unmatched anywhere else in history or in the world today. The rest of modern American journalism must be helped to live up to those high standards.